Away from War

Away from War

Florence Gordelier

The Pentland Press Ltd
Edinburgh · Cambridge · Durham · USA

© Florence Gordelier 1998

First published in 1998 by
The Pentland Press Ltd.
1 Hutton Close
South Church
Bishop Auckland
Durham

British Library Cataloguing in Publication Data.
A catalogue record for this book is available
from the British Library.

ISBN 1 85821 571 4

Typeset by George Wishart & Associates, Whitley Bay.
Printed and bound by Antony Rowe Ltd., Chippenham.

To my Family

Acknowledgements

I wish to thank my husband Ronald for his encouragement and support. Thanks to my children, Sandra for typing my manuscript and Patricia for giving me the confidence to put pen to paper. Thank you to Susan and John for keeping me on task. Many thanks also to David, David, Roger and Sandra, my children's other halves, for their continuing interest. Not forgetting my brother Bill, cousins Josephine (Dolly), Bill, Jack and June.

Thank you specially to my grandchildren for listening to my tales, for laughing and crying with me and inspiring me to write this book.

Contents

CHAPTER 1

Preparation for War

The year of 1939 was a traumatic one for me. Little did I know what was to happen over the next few months and years.

My mother and father were devastated by the fact that I had not passed my 11 plus. I was their only daughter and they had really wanted me to go to the High School either in Eltham, south-east London or in Catford, also in south-east London.

I was very pleased, myself, about failing as I was to go to the Council school at Downham (in 1939 Downham was in Kent). I would be able to walk to school or go on the new skates I had had the previous Christmas. But best of all, I would be able to go with my friends.

All the weeks and months of 1939 were a trying time for the grown ups, especially the ones with children. Talk of war starting with Germany was on everyone's mind. We had been having some really lovely warm weather all the school holidays. This was for me to be the last of my happy home life with my mother, father and younger brother.

All we could talk and hear about from neighbours and parents was war, war, war. That summer, instead of planning days out, most people with gardens started to dig holes. Most households had been allocated iron 'Anderson' air raid shelters. The men in the families would put them together in their gardens. They were told to wait for instructions.

When the time came everyone started to dig, six feet wide by eight feet long and about four feet deep. Sand bags were handed out and placed round the front. Then soil was covered over it. Grass seeds were set on the top.

The shelters were made as comfortable as possible. Single

1

mattresses were put in, spare blankets, pillows and cushions, all to make life a little better in case we had to stay in them for any length of time. We had a small camping stove in ours so that we could make a cup of tea. My mother had biscuits for us but most people had bread and jam. This was put in a tin and replaced every few days to keep it fresh.

Very soon it would be Easter. I had gone to look round my new school, Downham Senior Girls' School. My uniform would be navy blue drill slip, white blouse, and navy cardigan with a white and pale blue flash on the cuffs and collar. Also of course the dreaded navy blue knickers with a pocket in for our hanky. For PT (Physical Training) I had a short sleeved white shirt with navy knickers and a pair of black plimsolls – 3*d*. a pair from Woolworth's.

As the new term at school started, so strengthened the rumblings of war, although this did not affect us children. The Government had by this time started to issue all school children with gas masks. We were told they would save our lives if ever the Germans dropped bombs filled with gas as they had done in the First World War. We all had to have lessons on how to use these nasty-smelling ugly looking masks in a box. A few children at a time were told by teachers to go to class 1, to have a practice of these monstrous looking things. I remember the 'trying on' so vividly, even though it is now fifty-six years later. Babies were protected with a kind of pram top, covering them over. Children under five had a red coloured mask, with a red tongue on the outside. Although it was very much the same as the grown ups, with it being red in colour it made them look like an animal.

Mothers were told that, in the event of a gas raid, they were to put their own masks on first, which did seem rather a strange thing to have to do. Whether it was to help the children accept the mask if they should see their parents in theirs first, I do not know. The masks would be our life-line if the bombs were to drop, so we all had to carry them round our necks, tied on with string. Some of us covered the box with cloth to make it look more decorative.

Back at home the Anderson shelters were being finished in the gardens. Grass was beginning to grow on the top.

Whitsuntide came and went and the school summer holidays

were upon us. Talk of war was really hotting up. Parents were saying to each other over the garden fences, 'Are you sending yours?', meaning, were their children going away from home if war was declared.

September came. I remember it being the day before I was to go back to school. On the morning of 1 September, I heard a new sound, which was to live in my heart and mind forever, the wail of the siren. The siren warned us to take cover, the Germans were coming. But we were not at war!

There was a buzz in the air from everyone; all around was talk of war. That very same day over the radio were talks, telling people to start to black the lights from the houses. Black thick paper was sold for people to make blinds for the windows. Every household had its radio on all day and all night, just waiting with dread in their hearts for war to be declared.

3 September 1939. We all heard over the radio that war with Germany was declared. Yes! It really was war now. I knew I was to go to school almost as normal, but was told evacuation was to start.

My brother Bill, three and half years younger than me, was to go as well. Two boys about the same age as us were to go with us. They were friends of my parents and they wanted us to stay together. We were to stay together for a few months as the war wouldn't last long, everyone said. How wrong they were. I thought, how could I be responsible for three children, at eleven.

Talk of war and bombing by the Germans and fear of wearing gas masks made life rather busy for everyone. We had noticed large balloons in the sky, swaying on their ropes, looking like the big airships that had been seen in the skies a few years before. These large grey objects were known as barrage balloons. They were placed around areas such as Army barracks, factories, bridges, stations and around the coast.

I began to wonder what these barrage balloons could do. Dad said, 'They are to keep the German planes in the air so they can't see which targets to bomb. The balloons will stop the planes by getting them tangled in the wires.'

Several were near where we lived as we weren't too far from the Woolwich Arsenal. I did wish we wouldn't have to be evacuated.

3

Our neighbour's three children who were my friends were to stay at home and finish their schooling.

Mum started knitting on four steel needles some black wool stockings for me. Wool was still plentiful at about 1*d*. an ounce. When finished those stockings would be kept up with elastic garters. I had to sew the elastic to fit. I do believe Mum kept knitting to stop her thinking of what this war could bring. It had only been twenty-one years since the first war had finished. Now there was another one.

'A second war to start,' she said.

October 1939. Leaflets were passed amongst the children at school about being evacuated. Most of my friends were going to stay but as my father had lost his sight when he was forty, my mother thought my brother and I would be well looked after through the school evacuation, as people with a disability were going to be allowed to follow their children, as were mothers of children under five and pregnant women. But this was not to come until a few years later.

November came and my parents had a list of what we were to take with us on our trip to the country. It was made up like this:

First priority was the gas masks – with our name on the box.
A cardboard tag with our name and address on – this was to be fastened on our outer coat.
Toiletries – 1 hair brush (and/or comb), 1 flannel, 2 towels, 1 toothbrush.
A set of clothes consisting of – top coat, blazer, drill slip, 2 blouses, 2 vests, 2 pairs of knickers, 2 pairs of socks, 2 night-dresses (or pyjamas), 2 pairs of school shoes, 2 jumpers. (If you were a little bit well off you might have a dress or skirt and jumper, with Sunday shoes and socks.)

The clothes were to be marked with our names and put in a suitcase. I am afraid to say that my clothes were put into a brown paper bag, as were most of the children from the council estate and those not well off enough to provide a suitcase for each child. So that was it: all possessions packed in newspaper, bags and suitcases.

CHAPTER 2

The Time has Come

I remember it well, going to school with my parents to meet the teachers who were to go with us to the country or seaside. I was to go to the town of Cheriton, situated near Folkestone on the English Channel.

In November 1939, I aged 11³/₄, with my brother and the others were to go away, 72 miles from home.

The day came, early one morning, and we had made a packed lunch, which was bread and jam or fish paste sandwiches. We were to meet with others at the junior school of Pendragan. There I was labelled up with brown carrier bag and gas mask, ready to go on my charabanc ride to the Grove Park station a mile away.

Mother and Father came with us for the first part of the journey to see us off, which was rather an upsetting parting. Some children were clinging to their parents, and had to be lifted up the steps of the charabanc, struggling and screaming. Parents were weeping and cuddling their children for as long as they could. It was a long mile to the station. I had my face squashed up against the window watching my mother and father getting further and further away. I felt as if I was going to die. My eight-year-old brother was sitting close by my side. The two boys I had mentioned earlier were with me as I had promised to keep an eye on them, as we were similar ages.

At the station a few parents were waiting with their children clinging to them. They had been told to go to the train and wait. What a sad sight. Upset, crying children were tumbling out of the charabanc. Teachers kept us in groups of thirty to get on the trains waiting to take us to our allocated place of safety. The train journey is a vague memory now for me, yet after getting off the

5

station platform, we were to have another charabanc ride to a school hall in the town of Cheriton, Kent.

How I wished I could have a drink of water and wash my face and hands.

The hall was getting packed with grown ups, looking and staring at us. I was soon to find out why. These people had come to collect one or two children to take to their homes to live with them. The Government paid the sum of seven shillings and six pence for each child per week.

Several ladies took children away in twos and threes. I was lucky to be with Bill and our friends, two boys. A kind looking lady of about thirty, with a baby of about two, came over to us. We went with her in her car. We had never ever been in a car before as they were very few and far between in 1939. We were so happy to be taken to her home by car.

What a surprise I was to have at this first 'billet' (also called a lodging). We were to stay at this house for a few days until a more permanent house could be found. It was the first house I had ever seen with a coloured bathroom suite and blue and white tiles. Though we had a room with a white cast iron bath at home it was nothing as grand as this.

Our bath had only a cold water tap, and we had to heat the copper first. The copper was a large cast iron bowl set into house bricks with a chimney. A fire was made under the bowl, and water poured in from the top into a bucket then tipped into the copper to be heated up, either for a bath or to wash and boil clothes in. All white clothes would be boiled up in soap suds, then taken out with a pair of wooden tongs or even just a wooden stick, then put into the bath of cold water to rinse them. Coloured clothes were washed in a smaller bath and rubbed up and down on a wash board with soap. The wash board was made of wood ridged on two sides. It was rather hard work rubbing the clothes over the board. After rinsing, the clothes were lifted out, and either wrung out by hand or put through the mangle: two wooden rollers turned by hand by a wheel attached to a cast iron frame. The clothes were put through the rollers several times to squeeze out the water.

White clothes, before being put through the rollers, were placed in a bowl in which a small one inch round piece of blue coloured chalk wrapped in thin cloth had been put. This was called a 'Dolly Blue'. How the white washing sparkled, clean and fresh, in this rinse. After another session of putting through the rollers the clothes would be folded and finally they were hung out in the garden on a line to dry. So really my family were better off than some. A lot of others still had a tin bath.

Therefore to be in this house with a blue bath and toilet and basin, and blue and white tiles on the walls, and hot running water from a tap – oh! What luxury it was.

The four of us children were to stay in the 'blue house', as I called it, for only a few days. Our kind lady, with her baby, had a letter to say her husband, an officer in the Air Force, was to be sent to Canada to train some young Canadians for the Air Force. She would be able to go with him as he had relatives in Toronto.

We said our goodbyes. We were to go in many more houses before the war ended. We were pushed and shoved about, as I would say, 'from pillar to post'.

CHAPTER 3

Moving on

What a change the next home was! We were still together, we four. We were taken to the sea front at Sandgate, about three miles away from Cheriton. This was an awful experience for me as I was the only girl amongst nineteen boys all staying at this hotel on the beach (with no road to cross to get to the sea). It was an awful beach of shingle and stones.

Every morning, after breakfast of bread and jam with no butter, we all had to go for a walk on this stony beach, which for me was like being tortured. The only good thing was the sun coming up over the English Channel. I was so glad to get off that beach and to sit or stand in the garden of the hotel which joined on to the beach.

It was a large hotel run by two ex-Army officers. I cannot remember any ladies being there, only males. We all had duties to do, such as making the beds and tidying up. This seemed like an endless task as my brother Bill and I were very homesick. We stayed here for three weeks and did not go to school during this time, the four of us who knew each other.

The day came one Friday in 1939 when we were to move again. I will always remember Fridays. As the years have passed since then I have never ever liked to move on a Friday. The previous few days we had been hearing shelling coming from France. They were in fact not bombs but big guns firing over us at Sandgate. We children would not know whether they were from France or from ships owned by the Germans. These large guns were called in England, Big Berthas. There were no shelters in the houses on the south coast, either in the gardens or in the streets, until quite some time later, so we would look out at sea in wonderment at being shelled.

So we moved on, having seen no teachers or school for several months. The nineteen boys in the hotel who had all come from one school in London were now to be split up. We four were taken to a school on a bus (or charabanc, as they were all called in those days). It was a senior school at Cheriton, Kent. Not for lessons. Oh, no! It was to be looked over by prospective foster parents prior to being taken into their homes. My brother and I stayed together, but the two boys were taken back to London. I was never to see or hear from them again.

From the school we were taken to a house which was to be a very welcome home for us. This smart detached house was owned by Mr and Mrs Fergusson and their son Julian who was eighteen months old. They were a middle class family, with full time jobs, a better way of life than I had been used to and a black Ford car. We lived in luxury. Being very sad at being away from my parents I became a little rebellious. I had a lovely bedroom with a single bed with green linen sheets with the owners of the house's initials embroidered on the corner. What a lovely bedroom it was, decorated green, pink and white. My brother's room was the same but in blue, lemon and white.

Every morning by the side of the bed was a Cox's English apple for us to start the day with. Mr Fergusson would order eating apples and cooking apples by the bushel from Kent orchards. They were delivered by horse and cart from the farm in Cheriton.

Being nearly twelve, I was to start the senior school. I did so for only a few weeks (I will tell you why later). There was also rather a lot of work to do at this billet, even though a lady cleaner was employed to come in two or three times a week. I was given a list of my jobs. Looking back, these really taught me a few things. I had to make my own and my brother's bed. No clothes were to be left out or untidy – the beds were very special to the owner (Elaine, who was just twenty-two). The bed covers had to be straightened and pulled tight, ensuring the initials were seen, and the pillows shaken and smoothed. I then had to help in the main bedroom, which had the same initials on pink sheets. This bed had a flowered cover with curtains to match. How beautiful it all was. My job was to dust after the bed making. There were no chamber pots (or 'guzzunders' as we called them) as there was a toilet and bathroom next to the bedrooms. My dusting job was to continue downstairs, into the dining room only. I was never allowed to do any jobs in the lounge. 'Lounge' was a new word for me; I called it a front room with armchairs in. I suppose there were too many glass vases and trinkets about for an unknown eleven-year-old to go near.

My duties also included looking after their eighteen-month-old son Julian. I had had no experience of handling little children. I would put him in his high chair in the dining room, and it was quite an effort just to get him seated, let alone spoon-feed him. His arms and legs were everywhere. For me to get a bib around him was quite a small fight, then to get him seated in his high chair with him kicking and screaming. Spoon-feeding was a process of one spoon in his mouth, the next all over the high chair and a little splattering on us both. I began to understand that poor Julian didn't know me. He had only been fed before by his mother. As the days and weeks went by Julian and I became on good terms. I cannot say friends, as he was too young.

Julian's father was lucky to be a car owner. How rich Elaine and Anthony were back in 1939.

On Sunday mornings Anthony would take my brother and me to the local beach near Folkestone, which was a few miles away, for a swim. The beach had no sand, only pebbles. Much to my surprise we would park the car on the sea front, and out we would get with our knitted swimsuits and towels. We could only do a few strokes at the local baths at home.

What I write now I do not feel was true, as most people would not believe it could be. But it is true, very true. We were to go swimming with no clothes on. We walked with great pain to our feet because of the pebbles. There were about ten men. They all dropped their trousers and coats and shirts. They waddled to the sea.

Yes! Yes! Starkers! Naked!

Anthony did the same; he didn't seem to think it was wrong.

Not for him, maybe. But for me it was awful, I suppose it was because I was a girl on my own.

So, every Sunday morning till Christmas we went. The weather didn't seem to worry the bathers. After Christmas it went on again. I had to take this as a new experience; there was no one to tell. No mum, no teacher. It was part of being billeted on a family we didn't know.

Back at Elaine and Anthony's home, although I had a lot of jobs to do it was very pleasant living with them. Elaine taught me how to knit, and how to peel and cook vegetables such as artichokes which would be eaten like a potato or made into soup.

I wish I could have stayed at this house longer, if only I didn't have to go swimming.

CHAPTER 4

Back and Forth

By Christmas 1939 my parents were beginning to miss us. Things were quite quiet in London; you wouldn't have known there was a war on. We were to go home for a few days. We would be back after the Christmas holidays (in those days it was only a two-day celebration. Christmas Day and Boxing Day).

We hung up our stockings, which were hand knitted in black wool, or Mother's thick lisle cotton stockings. In the stocking on Christmas morning to our delight were: an apple; three or four nuts, such as walnuts or brazils; two or three brand new copper looking halfpennies or pennies. There would be a pencil and a packet of wax crayons. Boys would have a gun that shot caps and girls would have a doll made of celluloid. Perhaps there were a story book and a game of snakes and ladders or ludo. We could have a Bingo game (Housy-housy or Lotto as it was called then). Food was limited.

After Christmas I was to go back to Cheriton, to live with Elaine and Anthony Fergusson to help look after Julian and do the house work. Sunday bathing continued right through the winter.

Everything seemed quiet after Christmas. There was no mention of war. I was due to start a lovely new secondary school. It would soon be my twelfth birthday, I was very homesick and a little frightened as the grown ups were talking again of war, bombing, Germans, France and Paris. The war was hotting up.

All the talk was true. The Germans had advanced towards Paris (and to think France was only twenty-four miles from our coast, where the Government had evacuated us children from London. There was only the English Channel between us and the enemy).

The Germans started to shell us from France, again and again with their huge Big Bertha guns. The shells could reach our beaches at Sandgate. We were all very frightened and we soon found we were back in London where it was quiet and safer. We had heard that France had given in to the Germans, who were entering Paris. We were on our own now.

During the summer of 1940, each day we would hear the sirens wail, sometimes early in the morning. The sound of the enemy planes would be droning overhead, and the English fighter planes would go up to intercept the bombers. The Battle of Britain started to rage overhead.

Some of the German bombers got through and went on to bomb London. The worst of the raids were when we were in bed asleep. The siren went and my Dad would get us to put a cushion on our head to go out to the air raid shelter in the garden. It was to protect us from the shrapnel that came down from the ack-ack guns with which our soldiers were trying to shoot the Germans down. Then an hour or two later the 'all clear' would sound and everyone would go back to their houses and carry on in their usual way.

By now rationing had started. This was per person:

8 oz sugar a month
Sweets were not rationed until about 1942 – then to only 12 oz a month
2 oz of butter a week
2 oz of lard a week
2 oz of cheese a week
2 oz of tea a week
Fruit was scarce, there were no oranges though we could get a few English apples that were available. Bananas were available for children under five – 1 per month
1 egg per week
1 lb jam a month

Every evening we would hear the drone of the German bombers who were on their way to London to bomb the Woolwich Arsenal or the docks on the Thames. The sirens would sound that awful wailing noise, dreadful, even though it was a godsend to let us know the bombers were on their way. We would look up to the sky and see our RAF boys going amongst the German planes. Then the German Luftwaffe would go into battle in the skies of southern England. One German escort plane came down and was broken in pieces and the next day everyone was out looking for pieces of plane. We children were looking for the pilot, but he had landed in a clump of trees and was rescued and taken prisoner by two ARP members. These ARP people were mostly men who were too old to go in the Army, Navy or Air Force. They were given, by the Government, helmets, jackets, trousers, and a stirrup pump which was very much like a bicycle pump only larger. It could be put into a bucket or container of water to put small fires out. The full title for the ARPs was 'Air Raid Protection Officers'. They lived in their own houses but had meetings every month to keep them informed of any changes in the war effort. The Home Guard was formed as a home army, and older men volunteered for it.

Many of us children would go around the houses and collect newspapers, which we would take to a shed or someone's dry area. They would be tied up in bundles, to await collection to go to a factory and be recycled into more paper.

In June, I was still at home with my parents. At odd times of the day the sirens would go, and we would all go to the Anderson shelter. There had not been a lot of bombing, just a few German fighters, and our aeroplanes would go up and have a few dog fights (as they were called) over our heads.

By the middle of June 1940, London had been bombed. The race was on again for children to be evacuated. I had not been to school since September 1939, yet I was to go to the school again with my brother to be evacuated once more. I had a bag with the labels on my clothes the same as the previous evacuation. Gas masks hung round our necks and up to the school we went again.

We were being told we might go to Canada, as lots of people could go if they had relatives to take them (which we had). It was however a very dangerous time as the children and some grown ups would be taken to Canada on cruise ships and the Germans would bomb any of their enemies, so it was not considered a reasonable option for us.

There was a six day push to get the evacuations going again. London had been bombed and on one terrible occasion in one of those London raids, I had heard that my mother's eldest brother Thomas, his wife and my two cousins had been killed as a bomb had made a direct hit on the London British Legion Club. My Uncle Tom was a Commissioner, so he was on the door in full military uniform. It was a special day for the British Legion, as there were men and ladies, members of the Legion, having a celebration party. Over a hundred people were killed or injured that night in the bombing of London.

So the evacuation was to start again.

We were this time to go to Northamptonshire in the heart of the British Isles, not on the coast as before.

I had my two carrier bags, which were not plastic as today. Plastic was unheard of fifty years ago. The bags were made of strong brown paper with string handles and inside were socks, knickers, nightie and so on. Knickers were always navy blue or green with a pocket and elastic threaded through the waist and legs. The legs would come to just above the knee. This was quite uncomfortable especially if you had chubby legs like mine.

Mum still went on knitting black stockings which were kept up with garters. (My mother also knitted me a swimsuit; it was fine until it got wet, then it would hang off me like a big wet blanket. The gusset stretched when wet almost down to my knees.) Boys wore the same elastic garters for their socks. They could be bought from haberdashery shops. The haberdashery shops sold all sorts: cottons, needles, tape, ribbons, and men's and ladies' clothes – mostly underwear. The garters would cost about one penny a pair. Yet a yard of the same elastic would only be a farthing (four farthings to a penny).

One carrier bag being full, in the second I had a pair of plimsolls. (Plimsolls were mostly black and were used as slippers, unless of course you were well off enough to have slippers). I had a pair of white plimsolls as well as black. Every day after use I would clean the outside, making them white again by using a block of whitening. With a piece of cloth and a little water rubbed on the block of whitening, you dabbed it onto the plimsolls. They would look like new again.

Woolworth's would sell plimsolls for 3*d*. a pair. Everything in Woolworth's was sold under 6*d*; nothing was ever more. You could buy articles in two, three or four pieces, each piece being 6*d*. It was known then as the 3*d*. and 6*d*. store. A pair of shoes would be sold in two parts, 6*d*. each shoe. A fender of tin to go around the hearth of coal fires would be 6*d*. each part as they were sold in two halves. It was a store that sold everything any household would want, except furniture. Many shops would sell their wares for a penny, and farthings and halfpennies were used all the time. Prices were shown as 1^1/4*d*., meaning 1 penny and one farthing. Socks cost a penny three farthings, shorts would be sixpence. Even these prices were expensive as wages were only around ten shillings a week.

I also had two books with me, a dictionary and *Little Women*.

Evacuation day came again. This time I covered my gas mask with some red American oil cloth. This cloth was very widely used, especially for table cloths as it saved time washing. Shelves were also covered with it to make them look more attractive. Some of the patterns were quite pleasing. A wipe over with soap and water and they would be as good as new and last for years. Some people even covered settees and chairs. It was good and hard wearing.

All clothes that hadn't been previously marked were done with indelible pencil. We had our sandwiches packed for the day. As before, I had bread and jam, spread very thinly so I wouldn't get sticky fingers.

The second day of my evacuation was again a charabanc ride. We were taken to the same London-Kent borders station. The destination was a village in Northamptonshire called Middleton Cheney.

The train was very crowded with school children, teachers and a few parents and grandparents. As we were so crowded on the train, one teacher to forty children, we sat three or four on a carriage seat, all with our bags, a very few with suitcases. Gas masks were in a box with string. What a pathetic sight: some whimpering, some crying in a really distressed state at being parted from their parents. For some it was the first time of separation, others like my brother and me for the second time.

The train pulled out of the station to the sound of grieving parents and children crying, some almost yelling, and lots of 'Goodbyes' and 'See you soon' to their offspring who were going to an unknown place to live. Of course we were going for our own safety but as children it was difficult to understand that.

Before we left the Church Hall we were given a warm drink of tea made by the church ladies in an urn, a large tin like a small dustbin with a lid on and a tap at the bottom which would hold about four gallons of tea or hot water. This was put on an open fire or a gas ring as there were very few electric cookers about. We also had cakes before our journey north.

There were eight or ten buses all lined up near the station in Banbury. I remember being upset and the teacher who we knew said, 'Let's all say together the poem . . .

> As we were going to Banbury Cross
> We met a white lady upon a white horse
> With rings on her fingers and bells on her toes
> She will have music wherever she goes.'

We all cheered a little, but not very much.

My little brother was very sad. He was tired and missing our Mum and Dad. He sat on the wooden floor in the school hall, very weary and tired. There was a lot of underhand talking and whispering (I thought at the time) while a couple were being persuaded to take us. We of course had no say in it. How I was to regret ever going away this time. The villagers seemed to take such a long time to decide what child or children they would have. We were all so tired and must have looked quite dishevelled with very little food or drink, not at all like the 1990s with crisps and cans of cola, lemonade and chocolate bars in a tuck bag. We looked like waifs and strays; we were treated like waifs too.

Standing there in the school hall feeling very sorry for ourselves, the younger children would start to cry for their mothers and fathers. Not that it would do any good with them

17

being over two hundred miles away. Time passed slowly on and there were only a few of us left. The girls were mostly chosen first, and always the girls with plaits and ribbons in their hair. That was to make a great impression on me. I would, whenever possible wear ribbons to match my dress, but my hair never grew long enough for plaits. (Instructions for plait making: take three strands of hair; with one strand in the right hand and two in the left, say to yourself 'right over left, left over right,' and the plait would be made.)

I kept thinking to myself, it must be nearly time for my brother and me to be chosen. At last a stout well dressed lady came over to us. She seemed quite snooty, but her husband looked quite friendly.

We hadn't got far to go as the school was in the middle of the village, just a few minutes away on the main road. The house was in a three-storey row of houses next door to a butcher's shop.

We were introduced to their two daughters and shown to our room. The room was at the front of the house, small but very nice and clean, with pretty wallpaper and a pink bedspread. Under the bed there was a po (or guzzunder) which made me laugh a little.

The days went by very quickly. There were quite a few things I had to remember to do. There were times when I wanted to run off. I was used to doing jobs at home with Mum and Dad, but these jobs seemed a little over the top. One such job was having a damp cloth and wiping all jars such as jam and marmalade that came off the table, before putting them back in the cupboard. Shoes had to be wiped clean and hair brushed outside. Hair had to be brushed a hundred times to make it shine.

I was given a bike and taken to Brackley by the man of the house to meet his relatives. I felt like one of his prize rabbits to be paraded. They all liked the way I spoke, being a little cockney girl. He did have lots of rare breeds of rabbits and I was to help clean and sweep the sheds. It seemed like every day but it was only once a week really. I didn't like this billet at all.

One unfortunate morning, I got out of bed to go to the loo. As the lavatory was down two flights of stairs and out in the garden, I used the chamber pot. As I sat down to wee, I heard an awful sound. No, it wasn't my plumbing body system. It was much worse: it was the sound of the china po breaking. I was terrified of the contents coming out onto the floor. I looked down; it was in two pieces. Oh!!! What could I do? I know I was rather a big heavy girl at twelve and never should have sat on it so heavily. I do believe it was already cracked, as I am sure it wouldn't have broken. I really didn't know what to do. How was I going to tell the lady of the house? I was crying for my Mum and shaking. Downstairs I went. Did she go mad! How she shouted!

I had a bucket of water and floor cloth to clean it up. It was very easy to do as there were no carpets, only lino, so it didn't soak in. This upset taught me never to cry over spilt milk again.

There was more upset to come in this household. I was to go to school for a few months. I went to school quite happily. Villagers would stop and talk to me. Some would feel sorry for us being away from home.

Before I say any more about school in this village between Banbury and Brackley, I will tell you about a very nasty episode at this house I was living at. We all played games such as ludo, snakes and ladders and dominoes, my brother and I and the two daughters. The games went a little too far for me. The man of the house said we were to play a new game of 'get the penny'. It was suggested I would be tied with scarves to a wooden kitchen chair. Pennies were put in various places on me, such as up my sleeve, down my sock, even in the pocket of my navy blue knickers. The pennies were put down my back too. Whoever was playing would have turns in feeling for the pennies and get marks for how many they could find. The man of the house played this on me too and would get the pennies from wherever he wanted. He always got the pennies from down my back, not from anywhere else, therefore he would win the game. This was an awful thing for me. I was afraid to tell anyone, especially a grown up. The games went on for quite a few weeks and I was very unhappy about it and said I wasn't going to play any more. But that was a very difficult thing to say and carry out when you are living in the person's house. I did tell a girlfriend of mine and we both went to our teacher, but nothing was apparently done about it.

19

Yet, not too long after, my brother and I were moved to another house.

This new billet was rather an exciting place. It was four stone cottages which had been turned into one. I had the end bedroom, a lovely single bed with white sheets and white quilt. I was given a candle and holder as there was no electricity. We had candles to see us to bed, then these were left on the small table at the side of the bed. There was no gas in the house either, only oil lamps. There was a large room with a very big wooden table with chairs round it.

On the first day we were all given a chair to sit on – I say all, because there were also two children and two young teenagers who were the children of the lady of the house who was a widow. I remember sitting at this table and being given my rations for the week. I hadn't had my own ration to look after before, and it was rather strange. 1940 had seen jam rationed: a one pound jar for four weeks. There were also ½ lb of sugar and 2 oz butter per week; 2 oz margarine; 2 oz lard; 2 oz of cheese and 4 oz of bacon. The sugar and butter had all been rationed before. Sweets were not rationed until 1942, when we were allowed 12 oz of sweets every four weeks.

In 1940, all the iron railings were cut down. Spare saucepans and other metal items were collected up to be put in a furnace for melting down to make guns and tanks for the war effort. All signposts at road ends were also taken away, just in case we were invaded by the Germans from France (it being only 21 miles across the English Channel). These things were happening all over the country. By taking down the road signs, they thought it would prevent the Germans from finding their way around the country.

Paper and newspapers were also collected by Guides and Scouts and sold for recycling for the war effort. Coal was rationed by 1941; some clothes were put on ration. Everyone was supplied with clothes coupons and ration books. We all had an identification card with our address and an identification number. Buttons and bows were restricted on clothes. Utility was stamped on all items of clothes and furniture. Shoes were not rationed until 1943, when it was only two pairs per person per year.

It was a must for all windows to be taped in a criss-cross fashion, to stop the glass shattering in the event of a bombing raid. There were sand bags put around buildings to protect them from being shattered. Church windows were boarded up. The sirens went off at various times, but I thought it was more often for practice.

The ARP men were around; usually one lived on each road. We all had to be so careful when it was lighting up time. The windows had to be blacked out with their dark paper roller blinds or thick curtains had to be pulled together before the light went on.

CHAPTER 5

A Cottage Garden

Here I was at my second house of my second evacuation. I was very happy at this cottage. There was a lovely large garden, full of vegetables growing. I was allowed to get some of the peas and beans, carrots, potatoes and beetroot when they were ready. I would bring them to the back door in a bucket and wash the earth off the root vegetables.

Besides my brother and two other children all evacuated from London, a little frail old lady came to the house. She was the grandmother of the two other children. Mrs Taylor said to the lady's son who had brought her to the house:

'Can she do any little jobs as there are a lot of people living here?'

He said, 'Yes! She can wash up and peel potatoes nicely.'

Well! What a thing it was to see this little lady peeling potatoes. She didn't peel them very thinly, but very thick, so that job was taken off her, but she did do her share of the washing up.

The biggest job for me was making the rations reach out for a week. One of Mrs Taylor's sons worked on a farm, so he was able to get lovely fresh eggs extra for us. He also had extra rations of cheese.

Life worked out so well in this house, with us all doing small jobs in and outside the house. I wrote home every week and Mum would write back and tell us the news. Bombs were still dropping over London. We had heard that Nottingham and Coventry had been bombed; this wasn't very far from Middleton Cheney. I remember the night the Germans bombed Coventry. It lit up the sky as far away as us. Coventry Cathedral had a direct hit, and the whole town was blown apart.

Although upsetting, this event for me was a nice surprise. The Government were starting to evacuate others out of London, people such as mothers with young children and invalids. My father came into this category as he had had an operation which had gone wrong and so left him blind. He could only see grey and darker shadows. The Government would allow Dad and Mum to come and live in the village near us. We were delighted. I went to see where they lived, but I wasn't very happy about it at all. They were to live for six months in an upstairs back room in a council house. The room had a small cast iron fireplace with a fire which was lit every day to be used for boiling the kettle for washing, cups of tea and for cooking with a saucepan. The fire was also of course the only source of heat in the room, there being only a few radiators in the 1940s. They lived, slept and cooked in this one room.

On washday the lady of the house would let Mum go downstairs to a small building called the wash house to do her washing. It was a very sparse hard work affair. Soap suds had to be made out of a bar of hard washing soap, cut into fine shavings and swirled into the water. The clothes then had to be rubbed onto a wooden rigged board, up and down until they were clean. Whites were at this stage put back into the copper to be boiled up. This method of washing was used in the south of England but further north another method was used. A large dolly tub was filled with hot water. Water was still heated by the copper. To get the clothes clean a handle like a broom handle only small in length was used, looking to me like a three legged stool. If you were washing for a large family the washing would take all day. Then it would take days for the washing to dry if the weather was bad.

My family didn't like this small room to live and eat in although the householders were rather nice people.

Sundays were a very special day in this village as quite a lot of villages had evacuees billeted on them, living in their spare rooms. Some would do what the Government asked people, which was to save fuel. One of the save fuel ideas in this village was that on a Sunday, the local bakery would keep the oven hot, and people would take their joint of meat in a tin tray with a little lard to the bakery. These were numbered up and put in the lovely hot oven by the baker, to be fetched when they were cooked. There were of course no cars to take and fetch them in. Some had bicycles and would put the meat tin on top of the handle bars. This was quite a tricky thing to do, especially in the winter when it was icy on the roads and pavements.

I had volunteered to take the meat Mum had prepared for the oven. Meat was on ration by then so people only had a piece of meat on Sundays to eat, with left-overs on a Monday. The rest of the week people would have sausage or liver or hearts or tripe, the insides of cows or sheep and pigs. As well as the meat, Mum had whipped up a batter pudding. The batter would also have a number on it corresponding to the meat tin and would be cooked by the baker. On the way to the bakery my brother and I were arguing about who would carry the meat tin. We were going along the village when he kicked me, I kicked him back and in so doing the meat fell out of the tin and onto the pavement. Worse than this, the batter pudding went all over my coat and on to my shoes. What a mess this was, more so because we had to go back to Mum to tell her what had happened. She ended up taking the meat to be cooked with no batter. I was busy cleaning my messy clothes with water. We had to ask permission from the householders first, of course, to use their water. Before using any water you had to make sure there was enough in the tank, as the water had to be pumped up by hand from the well and then ran through the tap. No one seemed to want to do this job. Anyway I did get cleaned up and we did have Sunday dinner with Mum and Dad (even though Bill and I were having a share of their meat ration). How they grumbled about our fight in the village.

I was at the village school, in my twelfth year. Little did I know it was to be my last school days. The village school was very full with the London evacuees. My brother was in the infants and I was in the lower senior part. Some had arithmetic lessons in the hall taken by the headmaster. Sometimes he would single us out to answer a sum on the board. We would all be standing up as chairs and desks were in short supply. There were desks in the classrooms but not in the hall. My turn came to answer a sum which the headmaster had written on the blackboard. Chalk and blackboards were always used by teachers. It was on algebra and I had to find the circumference of a circle and I did try hard. But at that time I was unable to concentrate and so the other children would giggle at me. If I had been able to have a little tuition I would have mastered it. Those that got it wrong had to go back into the classroom and stand on their chairs for ten minutes a time. This kind of behaviour by the teachers was very upsetting for me. I suppose it was because, being evacuated, I thought they were just getting back at us London children for being there, making their school so overcrowded.

On one other occasion I had to do a talk to the others in my class about wild birds. So I went along the hedgerows and found a nest. I really thought it was a nest built by a bird, any bird. I didn't know each bird built its nest in a certain way with different kinds of materials. I found this lovely nest, and as I liked robins I did a talk on the robins and how they make a nest. Well! What a disaster that turned out to be. The nest wasn't a robin's nest at all; it was a blackbird's. How the locals laughed! I really think I had to do this talk in front the class so they could listen to my different way of speaking.

In needlework, which was a subject I rather liked, I had a habit of putting my needle in my mouth, between my teeth and lips. This horrified the teacher to such an extent that she had me out again in the front of the class, laid me on a low table on my back and with the help of two children pressed on my stomach while I had to say very loudly (with difficulty), 'I will not put a needle in my mouth.' I had to stay in this position until I had said it forty times. This was very uncomfortable whilst lying on your back and being held down and having your stomach pressed. I was in rather a distressed state after this, but over the years it put me in good stead, not to put anything in my mouth that shouldn't be there.

My family had come to the decision that we would leave Middleton Cheney and go back to Downham in Kent. Downham, now, is in the south-east London area. Mum and Dad took my brother and me back to London. We said our farewells to friends we had made. I was glad to see the back of the school, but upset over leaving the Taylors. She had been so nice and kind to take so many of us Londoners in. We went back by train to London.

CHAPTER 6

Back Home

The train was packed with service men and their large kit bags. It was standing room only in the corridor and we were packed like sardines. Mum and Dad soon got a seat as in the 1940s people were more polite than they are now fifty years on. Men would get up to let ladies have their seat, and children would stand up too. Older men would also have a seat given up to them. My brother and I were able to squash in the train carriage with Mum and Dad when they had been given seats. The train would stop many times outside a station, for no apparent reason, for ten or fifteen minutes, then off we would go again. This time it took five hours to get from Banbury in Oxfordshire to London.

It was nice to be home again with my own desk and books. I hoped to go back to school as things seemed pretty quiet and there were no air raids. At night in the sky we would watch the searchlights, like enormous torches, manned by soldiers stationed around the country. On the same Army sites would be very large guns on wheels and a turntable manned by soldiers. These large guns were turned towards the skies and when the enemy plane came over, the searchlights would get the planes in the beam of light. The ack-ack guns (as they were called) would open up with such loud bangs to try and shoot the enemy down. The wail of the air raid siren would sound out again. It took me back to the early part of 1940 when the sirens warned us the enemy was on its way with planes to bomb us.

In 1941 the Government was to put dried milk on the market for us to buy. It was lovely to make rice puddings or spaghetti or macaroni with it. The Americans were sending dried eggs to this country. No one would use this at first. Soon, though, word got round that dried egg was better than fresh eggs, and as we only got one egg a week the dried ones became very popular. Mum said she would be glad of a little extra milk and egg powder.

I had an errand to do one day. It was my turn to go to the local shops to fetch some fresh vegetables if they were to be found. Locals would sell their fresh goods to the shops. I would get brussels tops as they were cheaper than brussels sprouts, and only two pounds of potatoes as they were scarce. The potatoes were quite nice, well shaped ones. Farmers would have to sell all the misshapen potatoes they grew for pig food, and first the potatoes were sprayed with purple dye making them unfit for human consumption.

This particular day when I was helping Mum with the shopping, it was in the afternoon and the siren started to go off. How I ran home I'll never know, as too much went on that afternoon for everyone to talk about. We had all run to the Anderson shelter which was in the back garden. The drone of planes was getting nearer with the German planes dropping the odd one or two bombs. We could hear the whine of the bomb as it came through the air and the thud as it hit the ground. The explosion!! The glass breaking!! Windows were cracking even with tape cross-crossed over the windows. We prayed to God that the bomb wasn't for us, our name wasn't on it, we said.

I was the first out of the shelter after the all clear had gone. The sirens were placed on the walls of the fire stations and police stations. The all clear had gone and people that were home at the time crawled out of the shelters. That's what it was like: we were like ants or mice crawling out of underground burrows. I can't remember hearing this lone German plane. It was limping homeward, as you might say, flying low. The planes only had three men in, a pilot, a navigator and a gunner. This German plane came across from London where he had let his bombs go, having been hit by one of our ack-ack guns. He was flying very low and everyone near thought he was going to crash. They were flying over an infants' school just as the children were playing out and the gunner on the plane opened up his gun and shot the children with a machine gun. Twenty-three children were killed and maimed that dreadful afternoon. Some people said that as they looked up, the plane was so low they could see the faces of the Germans in the plane. The plane went on to fly out of hearing and sight, leaving this awful disaster behind them. We never knew if the plane even made it back to its base. Oh! Those poor children!

Life went on but we were all very upset and the sirens still sounded at dusk. I would be ready for bed sometimes, even in bed, when Mum would get us up and I would put my shoes and coat on over my nightdress. The ack-ack guns were going bang! bang! booming out as the planes went over. We would all have a cushion and place it on our heads to protect us from the flak which came from the artillery guns. There was one such gun unit only across the road from my house. This flak did a great deal of harm; if you were unlucky enough to be hit with it, it could kill or injure you. The flak would come down onto dustbins which were made of tin and make quite a loud crack. It would hit the roof tops and make holes, in fact it would do damage to anything it fell on.

I would go out as soon as it was safe and collect pieces of flak that were on the ground. The shells would make holes in or bring down planes if the shells caught them in the petrol tank, or hit the pilot. The gunners were almost always the first to be killed in a plane as they were at the back of them. The Germans had large bomber planes and also fighting planes which were smaller and faster; they usually came to escort the bombers.

Life wasn't very good at all for us; the rations didn't seem to go far. Everyone kept saying the war would soon be over.

Mum kept saying we ought to have stayed in Northampton as she was very worried about us being in London. Cigarettes were in short supply and coal was on ration of one bag a week. Later it was cut to one hundredweight every two weeks. Clothes were also on a ration and outdoor workers had a few more points as their clothes were used more and had to be washed more often. They also were the ones to get a pound of cheese and not 2 oz a week like us.

I had still not gone back to school like many other children. We were to stay at home. I really think parents didn't want to let us out of their sight because of the bombing raids.

CHAPTER 7

Life on the Farm

My grandparents from Camberwell had now been evacuated to Nottingham. With them was an auntie with three children, Bill, Jack and June. They all went to live on a farm on the outskirts of Papplewick village near the town of Nottingham. Auntie had gone there with her children while my uncle, her husband, was in the Army stationed in Ceylon (now called Sri Lanka). He had been called up at the age of forty-five. We had some lovely letters from Gran telling us all about this farm. The farmer's wife said there was enough room for her to take more into her house. They were wonderful letters for us still in Downham, with bombs still going off around us, and ack-ack guns going off day and night. So Mum and Dad said, 'That's it. We are off to Nottingham.' They made the arrangements, which I, being a child, had nothing to do with.

It was now April 1941. I had been thirteen in the previous January and school was still non-existent. I had only had two or three weeks of senior school teaching.

We were now on our way to the country. It was such a long journey. We boarded the local train from Grove Park station, Downham which took us to the railway station at St Pancras, one of the main line London stations. Another train took us to Midland station, Nottingham, but even then we hadn't finished our journey. We had to get on a small steam train to Linby village station, and then wait for a bus to Papplewick and Newstead Grange Farm.

Mum had packed sandwiches of fish paste and meat paste (both sold in small jars). Drinks were very limited: we had a bottle of Tizer and a bottle of water. Dad had a bottle of cold sweet tea; it was then normal for the working class to drink cold tea from a glass bottle.

It seemed our journey would never end. Poor Dad; it was a traumatic time for him as he couldn't see. Yet he did carry the case and drinks.

I had two bags with my own clothes in. Bill, my young brother, had two carrier bags. He also had one or two special toys he had been allowed to bring. I had one or two books, one being the Bible, tied up with string so that it was easy for me to carry them. Mum had her handbag and the food bag and she had plenty to do with looking after us two and also Dad, as he had to hold on to her arm and be guided along. We all prayed every day for Dad to be able to see. It was the worst thing to happen to anyone to go blind.

I was on another evacuation. This time it wasn't quite so sad. We had closed our house in London for a while. At least until the bombing had stopped, so we thought.

The double decker bus was taking my family and me to an unknown adventure. I had only seen the London red double decker, so to see a blue bus was exciting to be sure. I noticed more than anything that the iron railings were still in place around the houses. These had of course all been removed from London and the surrounding suburbs. I can remember them being sawn off and taken away by a horse and cart. Why, I wondered, did this not apply to the railings in this area?

The bus took us through the village of Papplewick and up the hill. The trees were so high and the road so dark, as the branches touched each other from either side of the road. It was like going through a tunnel of trees, it was magic. I was sitting upstairs at the front of this lovely blue double decker bus. The blue seemed to match the bluebells that were growing in the woods at the side of the road. My heart was pounding with the thought of perhaps being able to live near the bluebells so that I could pick them. The spinney was behind the tunnel of trees. The lady bus conductor shouted to us, 'Grange Farm.' We were at our stop.

The bus stopped right close to a large oak tree. I thought, this was part of Sherwood Forest where Robin Hood had roamed around in his day. Off we got.

We four were on the side of the road and, looking round, there was no farm and no people. We had to look for two stones painted white, and there they were, only a few feet away. There was no gate, just a lane, which seemed to go nowhere, only down a hill. Coming towards us were Granny and Grandad. Oh! How we laughed and cried to see them. We all walked down the hill, to find at the bottom this wonderful square large house made of stone. Just to one side were two small cottages belonging to the farm, which the farm labourers lived in with their families.

The farmer and his wife stood in the hallway. We were introduced to each other. The farmers were Mr Eric Tillson and Mrs Maud Tillson, and also living there was their big six foot three son Peter and his sisters Edith and Emily. They all had their own bedrooms and living quarters. We had a very large room to live in, with big armchairs and a lovely wood top table, which looked as though it had to be scrubbed as there was no polish on it. It was a proper farm kitchen table. Nine wooden chairs were placed round the table and a fire was lit in the black cast iron oval sitting room fireplace. One or two hand made rugs were scattered around. It really looked so cosy as the fire had been made up with logs which were burning brightly. There were several rooms for us to use, for there were nine of us evacuees. I remember thinking how kind they were, to let us live there, even though they were paid 10s.6d. a week for adults and 7s.6d. a week for children.

I was to share a bedroom with my cousin Dolly (Dolly was her nickname; her real name was Josephine), not a very large room but it had a lovely view over the rolling countryside. Dolly was six months older than me. My Mum and Dad were in a larger room and my brother of nearly ten shared with them. Gran and Grandad had a room too. Aunt Lizzie had to share with my two cousins, Jack and Bill, her sons, the eldest being thirteen and the other ten. They also had a sister of eight whose name was June. Her bed was to be put in our room, to keep us company, so they said, but really it was to keep an eye on us as we (Dolly and I) were full of fun when we were together although quite like little mice when we were on our own.

After we had put our clothes away in the drawers provided for us, we were shown round the house. They were very lucky to have the largest bathroom we had ever seen. It was one of the bedrooms that had been turned into a bathroom. It was so clean. The walls were painted green; there was green lino on the floor, a large white bath in one corner and a wonderful white sink on one wall big enough to have bathed in. There was a pull chain toilet, also white. I felt so small in this large room. There were two wooden staircases in the house. There had been ten bedrooms when the house was built, before they had turned one room into a bathroom. All the rooms were full except for one which was smaller than any of the others and near the back staircase. It had a large black bolt on the top part of the door. I hadn't really noticed this until my cousin pointed it out to me. I was glad our bedroom wasn't too near this room. What was the bolt doing on the outside?

We had a lovely tea of home-made white bread and jam. It was a lovely time we had sitting all round this table. The bombs and war seemed such a long way away.

I woke up after a lovely night's sleep in the soft feather bed, so white and clean. Breakfast was of the same lovely bread, for which we were prepared to wait our turn. We could toast it on the open fire which had the night before been backed up with slack. 'Slack' and 'backed up' were new words to be learnt as I was in the Midlands now. Slack was the dust and fine coal left after the miners had got the large lumps of coal out of the pits, which I was to get to know more about later. The 'backup' was two shovels of this slack which would be dampened down with water and put on to the fire before bed, so that it would slow burn all night. Next morning it would be lovingly poked all over until it came to life again. If it was sluggish, our parents would hold a sheet of newspaper right up to the hole of the fireplace. The air from the room and chimney together would draw the newspaper tight and make a draught, so the embers of the fire would glow red again. Often the paper would catch fire. What a quick move it would be to put it out! We would all have turns of getting the large toasting fork. Every house would have one especially for toasting bread near the red coals or morning cinders. If you were unlucky the fire would begin to smoke and your bread would be black and taste awful, certainly unfit to eat. Worse still, your slice of bread might fall off the fork and into the fire.

My first day on the farm was not to find the nearest school. No one mentioned school at all. The billeting officer came from the village of Papplewick which was about half a mile away. The billeting officers were usually people who were on the local council or church council. They took the job on, usually voluntarily, to find lodgings for evacuees who came to live in their area. We had one such person come to take all the details of why and how we were to live in the community. She would see about getting us six cousins into school. It came about that only the two youngest of us were to go to the local school, which was for the infants and juniors only, so the four eldest, I being one of them, were left and nothing was heard about school again, much to our delight.

I can remember not knowing what to look at first. There was so much to look at on the farm. The farmer's children were only too pleased to show off their lovely place, so they said. One particular place was not something to be showing off about. They took it as a matter of course. It was a small hut not far from our door of the farm. It was a large house so there were several front, back and side doors. The side door was ours to use and the elders had a key for it. I have remembered this hut all my life and can look back and laugh but it was no laughing matter when I was shown what we were to use. It was our lavatory. It was called a double yoker. There was a large hole in the ground that had been dug out many years before. The top of the hole was small and had a wooden side and front. On the top of this wooden sided box was placed a seat of wood, with two holes large enough for two bottoms to sit on. Two people to go together, to do their business. Newspaper squares of eight inches were cut up and a piece of string pushed through the corner of twenty or thirty pieces of them and they were hung on a nail near, handy for wiping your bottom. The newspaper, we were all used to. But not the double yoke toilet. My cousin and I would go together and take a candle and matches to light when we got there. We would laugh and laugh all the way there and back.

35

I had lots of experiences at the farm. Peter would take us to see the pigs, which were in the yard with the pig sties all round. How we loved the little piglets. We were allowed to pick them up and stroke them. I felt my heart would burst with such excitement. The mother pig, the sow, would scream and squeak at us holding her babies. There were several pigs in the yard just rooting about, turning over the cabbages that farmer Tillson had given them. The mother sows and babies were kept in their own sty for a while. Peter would say, 'Come on, let's ride the big pigs.' He would get on their backs and ride them; they would squeak and squeal, grunt and shake to get him off. Really, it didn't do the pigs' legs any good, I'm sure. I didn't like riding on the pigs. but I did have lots of time to practise throwing a hat to see if it would land on the pig's head (or tail). Whoever of us six children missed was the one to be pushed about in a wheelbarrow and tipped in the pigs' slurry by the big farmer's son, Peter.

War was such a long way off, though it was talked about round the kitchen table. How I loved to go into the Tillson's own kitchen. A huge scrubbed top table was in the centre. On the day Maud Tillson baked loaves of bread the smell of the lovely hot bread reminded me of my stay in Banbury, and the lovely little bakehouse I had seen the village bread made in. Maud made and mixed the bread by hand, not with a dough mixer. She made cottage loaves, round with a smaller round on the top. They were her speciality. She promised Dolly she could help her make them. Bread had to be made every other day. The smell of baked bread would waft through the house and make us all hungry. Dear Maud would give us two large loaves and we had some of their jam. We Londoners never did such a thing as making bread or making jam, not when you could get it so easily in the local shop at home.

It was all playtime for us. Each day my cousin and I would go off on walks round the farm. One such day we walked across a field with daisies and buttercups and some pink low growing flowers. We would pick them; I did love to pick the flowers and this field had plenty of them to pick. I walked into the field whilst my cousin sat on the fence. The grass was rather thick; it came over my shoes. I walked on, picking flowers as I went. When suddenly a large brown bird flew at me, I screamed and fell back shaking all over. Dolly came running to me and all round us were ten little chicks, of browny yellow colour. Then I was shaking with delight at seeing such a wonderful sight. Poor bird, I had upset her sitting with her chicks. The farmer told us afterwards that they would be partridges.

Every day seemed to be an adventure. On one Sunday, getting towards Whitsuntide, the farmer had said we were going to have visitors. There was to be a party of children from the town of Hucknall that had a Sunday School outing from their chapel. I went with Eric Tillson to help – well, really to look at what he had to do.

In a barn he got out four large three foot by six foot sledges. I had seen a sledge before at home but nothing so large as these wooden monsters. There was a length of rope fastened on the front. He dragged them out, two by two. How big and strong he was! He had hands as large as shovels. But he was a gentle giant. His son Peter was of the same build but more aggressive.

Whatever were they going to do with four sledges? No snow, even. They pulled them out of the barn and dragged them up to the hill, the same hill I had come down the first day. By now the excitement was too much for me, but all Eric would say was, 'Wait and see.'

All of us were out of the farmhouse and on our way up the hill. At the bottom of the hill was the farmhouse, to one side a large pond. We were all now at the top of the field and waiting. FOR WHAT!!!!

Shh!! Shhh!!! Listen.

We could hear singing, because it was a Sunday School outing and children were coming. The singing sounded like angels. I was a little afraid of what might be. But I was soon to find out. Chugging along were two open lorries with 'Harry John' written on the side. The lorries belonged to a local firm which dealt in the transport of bags of coal or coke, cement and tarmac. The lorries had been washed down and the chapel seats had been put in rows so the children could sit on them. There must have been between eighty and a hundred children and a few grown-ups on each lorry.

What a sight it was. The children tumbled out of each lorry and just took over our quiet little part of the farm. Half a dozen men started to unload and there were boxes of food. Cakes and cobs had been provided by the local baker. In a quiet corner the food was piled up. Next to be set up were the trestles, folded down long tables. The chapel forms were placed nearby, so we could sit and have a picnic. What was very interesting was a large copper, placed on a stick fire that Eric had made. Very early that morning he had got the fire going so there were embers ready to put the copper on. It was filled with water from the pump outside the farmhouse, so the tea could be made.

What a lovely day it was. Cups of tea were freshly brewed over the outside fire, and sandwiches of jam and potted meat spread. The cakes were lovely too. They were to become my favourites. Coming from the south though I had never before heard of Eccles cakes. They were pastry with fruit mincemeat inside and sugar on the top. There were cream slices, which was again pastry cut into oblongs, spread with jam and cream with another slice of pastry on the top. To finish it off was a white glaze icing. These were new to me, as the southerners would have doughnuts or a pastry case with jam and then an almond flavoured cake substance. This was topped with icing and finally coconut strips. The strips were one or two inches long, like match sticks. These were called cheesecakes.

This Sunday School outing was really entertaining. It was a picnic and sports day all in one. Cricket teams were set up, sack races were taking place, running races too. Best of all were the 'sledge runs'. Everyone, young and old, would queue up to wait for their turn. The four sledges were pulled to the hill top, and then they would slide down the hill with four children and one older person. The grass was very short, the soil was hard, and the sledges went down the hill like rockets. We all screamed as we had to hold on to each other. The wind blew in our faces as we went racing down towards the pond at the bottom. Most of us were safe on the sledge, but a few nearly went into the water. There was always someone at the bottom ready to catch anyone who fell off. Some boys rolled off at the bottom for fun. Over and over again the sledges were pulled to the top of the hill. There was pushing and shoving and arguing and laughing, all trying to get on the sledge. My thoughts were for the children who did roll into the water and get wet.

We almost forgot we were at war, it seemed such a long way off, although there was rationing of food all over the country.

Whatever would their mothers say? It didn't seem to matter as the lovely day wore on. I didn't know any of these children who had come for a day's outing, so I was a 'looker on' along with my family. We were invited to take part in the games and they also shared the sandwiches and cakes with us. They were the best cups of tea we had ever tasted. There were no plastic cups like today; the chapel cups and plates were all made of pot and brought along with the coppers for tea. The tea was made in the largest aluminium teapots I had ever seen. Each of them had to be held with two hands. I was told they held a gallon (eight pints).

These chapel organisers knew how to cater. I suppose it was a regular outing, and they also had get togethers in the chapel hall. I had no knowledge of this as I was Church of England.

I was having such fun looking at the races, and I was able to join in with some of the singing of the hymns. At 4.30 though I heard a ring ding ding of a bell, and a great sigh went out from the crowds. The bell ringing meant it was home time.

Most people helped to clear up any paper or objects lying about and took it over to the lorries. The trestles were folded down (wiped clean first, of course) ready for the next adventure. The chapel forms were put back in the lorries in rows. Everyone got back on the lorry and had to sit where they had sat before. They seemed to be rather a rough looking lot to go back home. When they had arrived they had been all spick and span, with clean shining faces and clothes.

I felt rather sad not going with them. The lorry engines were turned on and they started to chug their way up the hill. I called it my hill, as so much seemed to have happened since that day at the end of April 1941 when I had walked down it.

We evacuees all looked on, waving goodbye, along with the farming family. We all wondered, would we have to give the lorries a push to help them get going? No, we didn't. What a sigh of relief I gave as I heard the children singing again. This time it was the lovely old hymn 'All Things Bright and Beautiful' that I had heard when they first came over my hill. But the words sounded like:

'Vote! Vote! Vote! for Harry Johns,
if you don't vote for him we will kick your door in.'

The lorries belonging to Harry Johns had brought the children and others for a lovely magical day out and that was their thanks. What naughty children!

After all the excitement of the day Eric said he would get Peter to put the sledges back in the barn ready for the next time.

The days turned into weeks, and there was no mention of school. Each day on the farm was an adventure to be sure. Eric must have had a brainwave. He called a meeting one evening for his family and mine. The meeting was rather interesting. Eric put a few ideas out for us children to do.

My grandfather had gone out to Nottingham on the bus and found a job at the local brewery of Shipstones. He was a drayman's helper. He sat at the side of the man who drove the horses, the drayman. How he kept those two large horses in check was unbelievable as he was seventy-four. The cart, or dray, would be loaded up with barrels of beer. The barrels were made of wood and iron, and full of beer, must have been so heavy for the two great horses to pull, yet they did with little effort. So my grandfather had a job and he was the only one working full time. He was able to get the job as most of the local men were in the forces. Grandma was to look after the chores and my poor Dad, being blind, was unable to do very much. It was the greatest upset of mine and my family's life.

My mother and aunt went into the village which was half a mile away to look for work. As there were several large houses in the village they were welcomed. They worked for two or three mornings a week, sweeping and dusting and cleaning silver. The wage was 1s.6d. an hour. Three shillings for two hours' work wasn't too bad, unless of course, some of the jobs included scrubbing the kitchen or the wash house floors. The floors were made of quarry tiles or flag stones, which took a lot of scrubbing on your hands and knees. If you had a kind employer, you used *warm* water, a scrubbing brush and a piece of Sunlight soap. (Sometimes there was a hard green soap especially used for scrubbing floors.) Sunlight soap was a cream coloured soft bar of soap, mostly used for washing clothes. Mum and Aunt Lizzie would meet each other after doing their chores and walk back from the village up a hill, my hill. It was a main road but the bus only came every two hours, so walking was the best, quickest and cheapest.

Mum and Aunt Lizzie would walk past the wood which we had seen from the bus on our way to the farm. No bluebells now, they had all gone, April as well.

We had all sat round for tea. A knock came at the door, and it was Eric. He said, 'How would you like to do some work on the farm?'

My Dad said, 'What sort of work and what about pay?'

Eric said, 'I suggest you get sixpence a day.'

Dad gasped, 'That isn't enough.'

Eric said, 'They are only kids and will take a lot of looking after.'

Eric was really on to a winner, which at the time no one noticed.

The children included my two boy cousins Jack and Bill (their young sister June was too young and had to stay with Granny). There was my cousin Dolly, and I. We had no special clothes, and we always had our black plimsolls. We were all set to start work the next day, after a lovely night's sleep in the soft feather bed.

CHAPTER 8

Working on the Farm

I am starting this chapter to describe a Tuesday as the Mondays were taken up with washing which everyone had to help with.

I was up early, as all country folk are. I really wanted to get into the swing of working and getting paid. We all met outside. It was about the end of May, and the sun was just coming up. 'Looks like being a grand day,' said Peter with a funny smile on his face, looking at us Londoners who had hardly seen a field before.

We had all been given a bottle filled with water for drinking, but no food. Eric and his son had a bottle of tea, which was also cold not long after being poured into the bottle.

We all sang 'Hi! Ho!, Hi! Ho!, It's off to work we go.'

I had been given orders to make sure all the gates were fastened up after we passed through, just to make sure no animals got into the other fields.

We got to the field which we were to help weed and to strike out ('strike out' meant to take out every other plant). The plants were swedes, which had grown from seed and were about three or four inches in height. Eric had given each of us a hoe (a hoe is a long broom handle with a metal spade-like tool on the end of it). I held it with a great deal of trouble, as to me it seemed so awkward, but I soon got into it as I thought of the payment at the end. We each had a row to do, starting at the side of the hedge and working down the rows of plants. Chop! Chop! you could hear; no one was singing or talking, only the sounds of the six hoes chopping at the ground. 'Don't forget,' shouted Eric, 'every other swede plant wants chopping out.'

Whew! I looked up and all I could see was field after field of green plants, rows of them. I didn't think much of this for a lark

42

(which is a cockney saying for not thinking very much of what you were doing). What a back aching, side aching job. No wonder Eric wanted help! We had heard the children from the Sunday School outing call him a 'slave driver' in a nice sort of way.

The sun had got up. I was so hot; my water had all gone. It would soon be one o'clock, which we had been told was all we had to work till. Well, until we got used to it.

The days came and went. I still got up early and filled my bottle with water. Off to the fields again. Day after day. There were millions of plants that had to be weeded out. My back wasn't too bad, and no one else complained too much. It never seemed to rain, so we couldn't have a rest. A rest never came into the slave driver's mind. I suppose we would have worked, even in the rain.

I had got up early as usual one morning. We had all gone together, and could see each row that had been done. I started, chop, chop, chop, with the hoe. The hoes were very sharp, being sharpened each morning before being used again. I chopped once too hard and as I only had plimsolls on, I cut my toe. I went down on the ground like a light gone out. Of course I was told afterwards that I had fainted. I wasn't taken back to the farm. Oh! No! Only just laid in the hedge bottom till I felt better, to start work again, I suppose. My toe being cut did get me out of the swede hoeing.

The evenings were getting longer and Peter would let us all have a sail on the raft he had made to go on the pond. He had a long pole which he used as a punt to push across the pond and back. The raft, roughly made but very sturdy, would take us one at a time and Peter as well. How I really enjoyed being here, no thoughts of war at all. No sirens going two or three times a night. No planes buzzing about, not even the rationing of food was mentioned.

Home made bread and hand churned farm butter was made. We could have eggs every day if we wished, not just one a week as the ration was. There were fresh caught rabbits, shot by Eric. The rabbits were shot then had their insides cleaned out. Eric and Peter would make a great delight of this, splitting the rabbit's underbelly and pulling out all its insides. I just stood with my hand over my mouth and only a couple of fingers over my eyes, so I could see. I really felt so sick at such a sight. The rabbits were then hung on two nails by their back legs and with a sharp knife to one leg the skin was pulled off. The skin was pulled over their heads. 'Oh! Oh! No! No!' I would cry. Eric and Peter just looked at each other.

'You be pleased when rabbit is cut up in pieces and cooked with spuds and onions,' they said in their Midland accent.

Then he sold the rabbits' skins.

One day Gran was given a chicken. This was roasted in the farm kitchen, not ours, as it was a sitting room fire that we had. What a wonderful smell it was, roast chicken. Maud said there would be many more if we liked, but she would have to charge us a few shillings for them. So for many weeks we had boiled or roasted chicken and lots of chicken soup with potatoes, carrots, onions and swedes. The chicken season was in because the farmers would clear out their hen houses of all the older hens. If you had over ten chickens the Government made you register with them and all the eggs had to be stamped with the date on each egg. They were wiped clean and put in trays for the Government egg marketing board to collect. They did pay for however many eggs were sent, but of course some eggs were kept back for family use.

As life went on in the farmhouse, so I and my cousins did more jobs on the farm. One day I had to sweep clean the horse stable. Dolly asked if we could get permission to ride on the horses. It was a wonderful idea and we were given an odd afternoon when the horses weren't being worked. We had no saddles to use as the horses were cart horses. We did, though, have a bridle to hold and the bridle was joined onto a bit which was in the horse's mouth. The bridle was pulled to the left or right so the horse would know which way to turn.

I had a lovely brown horse, my cousin a big black one. The farmer said they were gentle if you treated them so.

The sun was out, the sky was blue and we walked the horses out of the stable into the yard. We walked alongside them until we had gone through the gates which had to be opened and closed properly. The field ahead of us was our swede field, looking very healthy. It was close to a private lane which ran from Papplewick Hall, where the squire lived, to a lodge and gate, then the lane wound on to Newstead Abbey. We were to visit that later, Peter had said.

There was a nice flat grass field that was used for cows to feed on. No cows were there that day; we were to have a practice horse ride. I climbed on a fence to sit astride the horse and Dolly did the same. But she was heavier than I and had a terrible time climbing on the fence and holding the reins and getting one leg over the big black horse. Peter came from nowhere and was able to help us both get on comfortably. Off down the field we went, first at a walking pace, then I gave a dig with my soft shoes to the horse's side and that got good results. Both horses started to trot, then run faster. By this time I was holding the horse by the neck, holding on for dear life. Unfortunately I slid off onto the grass with a bump and my lovely brown horse just snorted as much as to say, he'd had enough of that. I was lucky to not have landed in a cow pat as they were all over the field.

We had many happy days on these horses, if, of course, we could get the time off as the farm working hours got longer through the summer.

I really wanted some trousers as a skirt was unsuitable for farm work. Maud suggested we went in to Hucknall on the blue bus, which was a two-hour service though early and later in the day they would come every hour. She said there was a shop which sold men's overalls. So Dolly and I went to town and we bought these lovely navy blue overalls which had a bib and brace and we wore our white blouses under them. We also had been given some new heavy shoes, which the billeting officer brought us, along with new coats and suits for the men. These were all free.

How Dolly and I strutted about in our bib and brace overalls and strong shoes. Our first day we went down to the village to show off. Dad said he would come for a walk. So up my hill and down towards the village we went, past the bluebell wood where the trees met overhead and made the tunnel. Dad had us two girls one each side of him. We would whistle as we went. The song went:

'With a shallaly under my arm
and a twinkle in my eye.
We are off to Tipperary in the morning.'

(We would change 'Tipperary' to 'London' in the morning)

Down to the village shops we went to see if we could buy a few cigarettes and perhaps a bar of chocolate, as we did have our sweet coupons. On our walk to the village shop we passed several large houses. I kept wondering, was that the house Mum worked at? I suppose it must have been, as she moved on to several houses in the village. The only reason for moving on was that the man in the house was called up and the big houses had to be closed up for the duration of the war.

I loved every step of the way. The village was such a vast difference from the council estate in London. I passed the gates of the Hall where the local squire lived, which looked very grand. It was set in a field of well cut grass. The grounds seemed to go on forever. It was the railings that really upset me as they were there, not like ours that had been cut off for the war effort.

There was a lovely row of cottages all built of grey coloured stone with tiny windows and painted wooden doors. They had the neatest gardens with roses growing round (not in flower yet as it was too early). I went past the billeting officer's large house and looked through the garden gate to see neat lawns and borders of flowers in bud. There at the side of the house was a lane, to nowhere, I thought, but a notice said, 'This way St James Papplewick Church'. I would look at that later, I decided, as all my present thoughts were, I hope Dad gets a packet of fags and that the shop has some chocolate toffees, which I liked.

We three felt a bit strange going into the village shop for the first time. It was a post office as well. The lady behind the counter was a neat looking person with a crisp white overall and her dark hair pinned in a bun at the back. She was very friendly and asked us who we were. I was the first to chime up, 'We are Newstead Grange Farm evacuees.'

I thought she seemed a bit taken back, as really Londoners weren't very welcome. One of the villagers came into the post office side, for some stamps, I suppose. Her husband came out, as he was the post master.

'My name is Amos Milner and this is my wife Ada,' he said.

We three said, 'Hello there!' almost together. 'We'd like some cigarettes and sweets,' we said.

He pushed his cap to the back of his head and said, 'Is there any, Ada?'

From that first meeting in the shop, ours was to be a very long friendship.

My jobs on the farm seemed to me rather enjoyable. Eric Tillson took us every morning to do some job or other and he did pay us sixpence as promised. The afternoons were filled with lots of lovely adventures.

My cousins and I decided to go for a longer walk round the farm. There was only a very rickety wire and wood fence to step over. What delights! I could see primroses everywhere, although I didn't pick them as they looked as though they were past their best. I thought I would come again another year.

Perhaps this was Sherwood Forest where Robin Hood and his merry men roamed. Yet I knew it could not be because the trees were only thin and spindly, not the great big oak trees I had read about in books of Sherwood. I read several notices up, such as 'Trespassers will be Prosecuted'. The wonders of the wood were before me and in front of me was open space and the sun was glinting on some water. A board was up which told me it was

PIKE LAKE

Private

Along the lake edge I walked with my cousins. There on the lake was a boat being rowed by someone very familiar. It was Peter. We waved and shouted to him; he was having such a pleasant time till we Cockneys came on the scene. But he did row over to us and the boys climbed into the rowing boat for a row round the lake. They did get their shoes and socks very wet. Oh! I thought, how Gran and Mum will carry on when we get home! The boat didn't look very safe yet they were assured the lake wasn't very deep.

What could we do now, only wait and look for some wild flowers growing in the woods in the spring. What a lovely sunny day it was for everyone. Our walk looking for wild flowers took us to the other lake where Peter had taken the boat. He tied it safely and to my disbelief they were stripping off and going for a swim; they did, though, keep their underpants on. Only my older cousins could swim, so they just splashed about and kicked water over each other with sheer delight. We sat on the side and I wondered at the sight of the splashing water against the sunlight; it seemed to form small rainbows.

Dolly and I were soon to be a little bored with this boys' fun and we decided to put a stop to it, or at least tell them it was getting late and we had better get back for tea. We had a lovely evil idea. (Well, it was a lovely idea for us.) We would gather all their clothes up and hide them behind the trees. This we did, to our delight.

We stood back when it was time for them to come out of the water and how we laughed when the boys were all running around looking for their clothes. It did take a while to get dressed for them that day, and they were all dry by the time they had found them. We all went back together after a lovely time had been had by all.

Our days were really wonderful, going for walks around the farm. We would come back for tea and afterwards Eric had promised to tell us some of the history of the place and area. He started off by letting us all go to see the cellars of the farm. What a shock we had. There was a small (only three feet high) door at the end of a passage. A large key was produced and with great effort the door opened with creaks and squeaks, and a musty smell and cold air were around us. We had been given a couple of candles between us but we couldn't really see much. The walls were grey stone, very dry looking, yet the damp smell was there. On the stone walls were two large iron rings and a step or seat under the wall with the rings on. We were told that monks had lived in the house and any that had wanted to get away or wouldn't work, were put there, tied to the rings, for punishment, maybe for hours or days. I was the last to go in the room and the first out.

There was a lot to be said about ghosts as well as the monks that lived around there. The story went that from the cell-like cellar

underhouse, there was supposed to be an underground passage to
Newstead Abbey, which was about a mile away. Eric said he had
never found the entrance to the passage but he had seen the black
hooded monk. That made us all very afraid. We were also to hear
the tale of the white lady who had drowned in the lake at
Newstead Abbey. At every full moon she would float out of the
lake across the road where I had fainted whilst hoeing the swedes
and sugar beet. She was supposed to come up to the house for her
lover who had farmed there a hundred or so years before.

I and my family really tried hard not to believe these ghost
stories, yet the house seemed to lend itself to them. Looking back
after my year or so on the farm, I really wondered if Eric had made
the stories sound worse so we wouldn't wander all over the place.
All he wanted us to do was to do jobs.

The time was coming up for the corn to be cut and got into the
barns. The weather was so hot and sunny. We were all asked to
help. The morning came, but what we were in for we didn't know.

We had a bottle of water or tea and chunks of home made bread
and blackberry jam made the year before. The big brown horse
was out with his leather harness on. He was attached to the large
black horse. They were to pull the rusty looking machine, which
was the cutter of corn or wheat or rye or oats. This machine was
called a binder.

Those that were to help in this were all ready for walking up my
hill. The main road was at the top, and on the other side were the
fields of golden corn swaying in the breeze. 'Giddy up! Giddy!' we
kept saying to Robey and Dobey, who were going to have to work
much harder than just taking Dolly and me for a ride in the lower
fields.

Eric was able to ride on this iron machine. He must have been
very uncomfortable as there was just an iron basket for him to sit
on. We had to wait till he had gone up and down the field several
times. The iron machine would cut the corn almost to the ground;
the corn would go through and be bound round with string and
then was dropped out in sheaves. After the cutting and binding of
several rows we were shown how to pick up two sheaves at a time
and place them in stooks of about ten. How my back ached after

49

only doing five or six stooks. I looked back at the work I had done. Oh! my back! They all looked like rows of small wigwams. The stooks had to stay like this for several days to dry out. Everyone prayed it would rain, so we could have a rest.

It never rained; the hot summer went on for ever. There was still plenty of oats and rye and wheat to cut, much to my regret. After two or three days of drying out everyone had to give a hand at turning the sheaves. 'Not again.' I said. There was no giving up on this kind, nice, slave driver farmer.

The sheaves were now very dry from the hot sun. My arms would just go round one, but Eric tried hard to get us to pick two up at a time. My arms at the end of the day were all cut and scratched; my fingers were bleeding. It was the dried thistles that were the worst. Eric would not do very much about weeding the thistles out before they got large. Weed killer didn't come into gardens or farms as it does today. We all got sixpence a day for this hard work. No teachers or billeting officers came to see how we were.

I really wanted to go and find this Newstead Abbey which Eric had told us so much about, but I had to be very patient as there were more of the small farm jobs to do.

In the bottom fields the swedes and sugar beet had to be lifted out of the ground. Dobey and Robey had their harnesses put on, and were backed into the shafts of the farm carts. Eric took all us evacuees in his cart down to the fields. The swedes were all in big piles. I thought, I can see why we have been given a cart ride. It was to help Eric and Peter to get the root vegetable into the cart (which was another back breaking job). No mention of pay this time, we had just gone for the joy of riding in the horse and cart. Several days it took to get them moved up to the farm barn, to wait to be taken to the sugar beet factory to be ground down into sugar. The swedes would also go to market to be sold for the public to buy, or be kept by the farmers to help feed their cattle. Eric also had a horse and cart with milk churns on and each day he or his son would go up my hill to the top road and sell milk in half pints and pints to the two villages only a mile or two away.

He would shout 'Milko! Milko!', the villagers would come out with a jug and he would take the lid off his churn and ladle out a half pint or a pint, whichever was wanted. He would then write what they had in a note book. They would pay him on a Friday or Saturday. He took us evacuees one at a time with him on his rounds every day.

Late September 1942 came and Maud was to make a lovely harvest supper. She had baked bread all day and made lovely cottage loaves. These cottage loaves were made into large flat round dough balls and a smaller one placed on the top. They were so brown on the outside and so soft in the middle and crusty to eat. We had the bread with big bowls of rabbit stew; potatoes, swede and onions were cut up and all boiled together. Eric had shot the poor rabbits when he was getting the corn cut. He would bring them back, as I have said, and skin them and sell the skins and we would eat the rabbit.

After the harvest there was still plenty to do on the farm. Eric said, 'It was nice to gather in the corn early.' I didn't know why. So Dolly asked him what he meant.

The reply was 'Weell, it been a looovley soomer. So all carn and root veg been gathered in early September.'

We were satisfied with that, though Gran said, 'You had some good help, son,' or it may have been 'cock' as Gran was a real Cockney.

'Oooh! Arrr!' said Eric.

It was nice to listen to the different phrases and sayings of the Midlanders.

CHAPTER 9

Looking for Ghosts

Each day there was such a lot to do on the farm. I really wanted to go and find Newstead Abbey and the ghost of the white lady. I dared not go on my own. I was able to persuade my cousin Dolly, we were such an adventurous pair. Off on our exploits we went.

From the farm through the lower fields we went, closing the gates behind us so the cows and horses wouldn't stray. The lane was before us. Earlier we had turned left, which led us to the Papplewick Hall and village. This time we went to the right. Along the lane we looked all round us because we didn't want to miss seeing the white lady that was supposed to hover about the area.

A few hundred yards along this lane we came to a stone house to the right of us and in front of it was a very high iron gate, painted black and gold. It must have been ten or twelve feet high. I thought that it could have been melted down and made into tanks or guns for the war effort. This huge gate was padlocked but to one side was a small gate to walk through.

I felt like Alice in Wonderland going through the gate to the unknown. The lane was in front but on the right were rows of camouflaged Army tents and Nissen huts made of corrugated iron on a brick base, with soldiers sitting and standing cleaning their guns. They were so silent; they never looked up at us two thirteen-year-olds. It was so very weird. We kept walking on tiptoes past the tents, then past the tanks and more lorries. The soldiers were busy cleaning the tanks and lorries in silence. The trees were tall at the back of them so it gave an eerie feeling. I suppose they were practising to be quiet if the Germans came. This was the nearest thing to war I had had for a while, apart from a few bombs which had dropped on Nottingham. (We were all putting on a brave face with the rations though.)

We were to walk further on, as our main aim was to see Newstead Abbey. On the left side of the lane the grass was as high as a mountain. A little further on we came to this lovely sight of the Abbey. To one side was a large pond. Oh! The wonders of it! The Abbey seemed partly ruined and there were no doors open; they were all barred up. There must have been someone living in this area, though, as the grass looked so well kept. There were a few cottages scattered about on the side of an even larger pond.

Dolly and I sat in wonder and we heard a voice saying 'Here! Here!' It was a man's voice. We couldn't get away as we were sitting on the grass lawn of the Abbey. We decided to say 'Hello!' and to tell him we were little evacuees who had come for a walk to see his wonderful place.

We didn't run away from him. As we made an extra fuss of his dog, I decided to ask him if there was any history about the place. Had he seen the ghost of the white lady? No, he hadn't, he said. He had, though, seen a monk dressed in black with a three cornered hat, floating around the edge of the lake. So we had two ghosts to look for now.

The man and his dog decided to go home, which, he said, we should do also, but we were too excited to take his advice and so we walked around this beautiful lake. There were ducks swimming and quacking and doing a bottoms up to us. We laughed. They were really looking for food to eat. We sat a while on the stone benches, which must have been there when the monks were about. Perhaps they fished for pike, a large coarse fish with lots of bones in it. It would be salted overnight and eaten the next day: that is what our man with his dog had told us.

It was still only early afternoon and the sun was out so we decided to go forth on our exciting walk. There was a small gate ahead and on a notice board were the words: 'This way to the Japanese Gardens'.

One path was only about two feet wide. We decided to take it. On each side of it were trees and bushes and low ground-cover plants; some were in flower and some had coloured leaves which we had never seen before. Small streams ran at the side and under the path again. It was so silent except for the trickle of water and then a rushing sound as the stream tumbled over rocks onto a lower level. There were numerous paths we could take, and we just jumped from side to side criss-crossing the stream. In front of us was a wooden hut with a curved Japanese roof and we sat a while just listening to the babbling brook.

My cousin and I still wanted to see more and we decided to cross some stepping stones. The water on each side of us was much deeper than we had seen so far and we could hear a rush of water getting louder and louder. Whatever was it? Getting off the largest and last stepping stone we found a pond; it was small but very bubbling. Just in front of us was a waterfall as high as a house. We were almost turned to stone in wonder. The sun on this tumbling water was forming rainbows in the spray. We wanted to run into it as the day was so hot, so we ventured a little nearer, still on the path. We pushed each other nearer the spray. The path was on a level yet this waterfall was a wall of water coming from above. As we got nearer we could see a wall on two sides, with this path we were on running in between, and on the left side of the wall was a large open window. We walked on the path and under the waterfall and stood and looked through the unframed, unglazed windows. We were looking through the waterfall; what a wonder it was! I wanted to stand forever and look and look. Dolly was getting a little tired, yet wanted to see more. We carried on our walk past the colours of the red and yellow and silver leafed Japanese bushes and trees, out of the low wooden gate which we closed behind us. To keep the ghosts in, we laughed.

Walking on over a small sized lawn, we found another pond with a notice on the trunk of a weeping willow tree. The notice said: Monk's Stew Pond. Rhododendron bushes made a screen around, and we could just imagine monks sitting and fishing for their supper all those years ago.

We were to learn later that King Henry II had founded the Abbey and laid out the grounds, though not the Japanese gardens which were added later. Henry II had built the abbey for the Augustinian monks who lived there for four hundred years with only a few troubles. By 1539 however the monks were going through a rough time as part of the English Reformation.

The monks were not able to take with them furniture or any other valuable possessions and many of these articles were thrown into one of the ponds. Many years later this pond was pumped dry and there was a statue of a golden eagle in it. It was cleaned and taken to Hucknall Church and remains there to this day (1997). There were many oak chests taken out and cleaned and put in museums. Many families were to live in the Abbey, one being that of the late Lord Byron.

We were now ready for going back to the farm. We passed the lake with the ducks still quacking and swimming but there was another sound now. It was more of a screeching; perhaps someone had seen the white lady or the black monk ghost. Yet the screech didn't sound human. As we turned the path, in front of us was a peacock with its tail fanned out, especially for us, we said. We were afraid to pass by but he was more interested in a large brown bird which we asked about later and were told that the brown bird was a peahen. What a lot we had to learn! Dolly and I huddled together, walking as fast as we could past the Abbey, which looked as though people lived there, as there were heavy looking curtains up to the windows. We passed the ruins of the Priory, which was part of Newstead Abbey, and went out on to the main lane that led past the slow moving quiet soldiers sitting round their tents and the Army huts all painted green that blended in with the trees and grass and hedges. Through the iron gates, and past the stone built lodge belonging to the Abbey, in which lived a girl who we got to know quite well, and back along the lane through the Newstead Grange farm fields, making sure we closed the gates behind us. We got back in time for a well earned rest and home made bread and jam for tea.

We couldn't tell Dad and Mum everything we had seen; it was far too much for them to take in, we thought.

My days were taken up with helping Eric and Peter clean the cow sheds, the horse stables and the pig sties. Dolly would often stay to help Maud bake bread for us all. We weren't paid for any of these jobs, only the field jobs which were now coming to an end.

The darker nights were coming and there was still plenty to do all day, even if it was only to tease Eric's fourteen-year-old son Peter. Some days he would call for Dolly, saying, 'Can I take you out?' But I would follow not far behind. He would try and kiss her and she would say, 'I'll have to bring a box to stand on,' as he was over six foot tall.

On another day it would be my turn and he would say the same. 'Give us a kiss, Cockney kid.' I would grab his woollen knitted hat and throw it as far as I could, often in the pigs' muck and he would go in with his wellingtons (which he wore winter and summer). It was all good clean fun (though his mother wasn't very happy about the hat).

One particular night my cousin and I went to bed. It was about eight o'clock. We would lie and talk about the day we had had. We lay on our backs looking up at the ceiling and a round light appeared, flickering at first on the ceiling, then down the wall, then on the curtains. We were petrified. Whatever could it be? It moved about so quickly, hovering up and down the wall and curtains, then it floated over our head. That was enough for us! We screamed and screamed. I was out of bed first and ran to the door and then the round flicker was on my night-dress. We got the door opened and on the other side of the door was my young brother Bill, with a torch he had shone through the keyhole. All the family laughed, but not us two. We thought perhaps the ghosts had come to get us.

We felt very uneasy in the bedroom from then on, so we were to move to another, smaller, one. The very first night in our new bedroom, just as I had dropped off to sleep, my cousin woke me up and we were to lie awake in bed again, this time listening to noises up in the rafters of the house. It sounded like chains being dragged from one side to the other. Hours it went on, well into the night. We never did mention this to anyone at first. The next night it was the same noise. We decided it was birds coming in to roost. Yet there was no sound of tweeting or wings flapping. Perhaps it was an owl which we had often heard 'twit, twooing', sitting in the trees. Eric had said the owls nested in the woods.

Maybe it was the ghosts of the white lady or the monk dressed in black in the attic, or maybe it was a person who had been put up there as a punishment. Perhaps even someone who was mad had been chained up in the rafters, as it was so much like a chain being dragged from one side to another. I really had to ask Maud, the farmer's wife, if she had heard these scratchings and chains dragging at night. She smiled a bit; I thought she was going to tell me a secret. No! No! Not a word did she give away. Night after night it went on and we were glad when we were let back into our front larger bedroom, even though we had had the torch through the keyhole episode. At least that was real.

Dad and Mum hadn't heard any scratchings overhead but Dad gave some thought to it. He said it could be bats flying in and out at dusk to feed their young. We were a little satisfied with that.

Our days on the farm were soon to come to an end. The Tillsons hadn't owned the farm; they were only the managers, and Mr Tillson hadn't kept up the standard the owners wanted. Whisperings said the owners wanted it for one of their daughters and so the Tillsons had been given notice. It was doom time for us all. On Michaelmas Day, 25 September, there was to be an auction of the farm machinery, which was very ancient. All the cows and horses and pigs and chickens had to be sold, and some of the furniture too. The Tillsons had to rent a house somewhere and take only items of furniture that were suitable for a smaller house.

We evacuees had to be found another billet or go home.

CHAPTER 10

Castle Mill

Gran, Grandad, Dolly, Auntie and my three cousins were to go to live together in a very historic house named Castle Mill. One part still had the water mill to which boys were brought from London and other parts of the country in the early 1800s, to be slaves to the landlord who worked them to death. In Linby churchyard are the graves of about thirty-five boys under ten years old. There were two more parts to the mill. One was let to a lady and her husband who were to keep the garden tidy. The other part was made suitable for my family. They were lucky as several people had furnished it and pretty curtains were hung at the windows. It was a three storey place with a large garden. Apple and plum trees, gooseberry and blackcurrant bushes, seemed to grow wild. Roses round the doors must have been growing and blooming for years. They were soon to settle in, happy, yet sad at not being together as up on the farm.

My Mum and Dad and brother and I had to go to two rooms in the village. All had outside lavatories, but not a double yoker like the farm had had. We were soon to settle in the village. I never did go back to school; I would have been leaving anyway the following Easter 1942. I was never approached by anyone about school, although my brother did go to Linby village school.

Though I had thought we were getting used to the village life, it wasn't as happy as on the farm. The good food, Maud's lovely bread, the wild rabbit stews and roasts, the fresh eggs, potatoes, freshly dug swedes and green cabbage were a thing of the past. We also had the clothes rationing now to get used to. Clothes rationing had been introduced in 1941. There were coupons for a coat or a dress or a suit, undies etc.

Mum and Dad were very unhappy as the days wore on. They would walk through the village to see Gran and Grandad. Grandad was still working at the brewery. The dray horses had brass ornaments on the harnesses: what a sight they were pulling the big carts.

I would wander off as well, Dolly and I didn't see each other very much after the farm. I would go and visit them at Castle Mill as it was so heaped with history. History was a favourite subject of mine.

How we all grew to love the garden there. The roses were still in bloom even as late in the year as October. We were hoping the war would be over soon. The sun shone all the time and Dolly had asked me if I would like to stay with them as we were missing each other. The apples and pears had to be all picked off the trees. Some had fallen off as it was getting late in the year. Gran was able to put some in boxes to eat later.

I was to live with them for a while. We had some rather unnerving moments. One particular day it was the turn of Dolly and me to clean all the inside windows. The windows didn't open outwards like the London ones. These frames slid from side to side and were lifted out. They were rather difficult to put back, so Grandad would put them right when he got home from the brewery.

Evening time came and went and it was now bed time. We had pulled the curtains and there was no electricity or gas in the cottages, only candles in the bedrooms and oil lamps in the sitting room. Cooking was done on a black cast-iron range heaped with coal. It was rather cosy in the cooler days but much too hot when the weather was warm.

Dolly and I lay talking in bed about what we had been doing all day and how much we missed the farm and the ghost stories. Our beds were facing the window and we could hear a low ooooooohing sound like the pigeons we had heard in the woods. Suddenly the curtain billowed out like a large balloon in front of us.

Yes! Yes! It was a ghost this time; how we screamed and screamed. The whole family came running up the stairs. 'Whatever is the matter,' they all yelled together.

We were just able to tell them what we had seen and Mum went to the window to look. She pulled back the cream coloured curtains and turned to us laughing and saying how the window had not been put back and the wind had blown the curtains in like a ghost. The oooohing sound was not the birds or a ghost but the wind passing through the slate roof above.

What a relief!

There were several little upsetting yet exciting times we had at Castle Mill.

One day we had to have the chimney swept in one of the bedrooms. Most houses had small fireplaces in the bedrooms and so the chimney would have to be swept. Gran wanted to get a chimney sweep in to sweep them before the bad weather came. Most people had their own rods and round brushes that would be pushed up the chimney. Every three feet it went up another wooden rod would be screwed into the last one. It would be pushed up and down the chimney from inside. Gran was to ask the billeting officer where she could get in touch with a chimney sweep. The officer knew of a lady who would lend them a set of rods with a brush.

I was to find out that the chimney sweeping day was worse than washing day. I was now living with Gran and Grandad, Auntie and the children at Castle Mill. Mum and Dad and Billy were still in the shared cottage in the village.

Everyone had to help. First we rolled the rugs up and put them over a line outside (if it wasn't raining). Then they were beaten with a flat spade-like tool made of wicker basket. It did get a lot of dust and dirt out, especially if they hadn't been done for a year. Some of us had to help beat the rugs with a long stick.

The furniture would be covered over with sheets if you had any old ones; if not, newspaper was used. All the ornaments were then taken off the shelves and washed. A piece of thick cloth or sacking would be put up to the fireplace and held down with bricks. In the middle of the sacking was a hole for the person sweeping the chimney to place the brush through. One rod joined another until the brush came out of the top of the chimney. Grandad had the job of sweeping. He said, 'All you kids go outside and shout when you see the brush coming out of the chimney top.'

It was quite an event to wait for, we thought. But not for what happened: the brush popped out and flew off the rod end. The brush, being round and flat like a wheel, rolled down the roof. We all laughed till our sides ached. Well, not all of us. Not Grandad.

In one of the other chimneys the brush got stuck fast in the side of the chimney breast. We had to borrow a ladder and as Grandad was over seventy, it was a bit much for him to go up the ladder, climb on the roof and look down the chimney to see where the brush was. He had a broom handle to poke down the chimney pot. He shouted to us in the garden below to tell Gran and Mum, who stayed inside, to help push and pull the rods. Was there any luck with their efforts? They seemed to have been pushing and pulling for ages and they had to give up, hoping for the brush to come out of the top. But it had to be brought down, along with soot and pieces of brick which had been dislodged. The soot made quite a mess. Mum and Gran looked quite funny with soot all over them.

It was all swept up and nice soapy water did the trick of getting rid of the horrid black soot. We had no vacuum cleaner so it was all cleaned by hand with a soft broom and brush and dustpan, then washed over with several buckets of water. The rugs would be put back and the ornaments placed where they had been before. The rods were wiped, cleaned and rolled up in a sack ready to be given back.

The next thing was everyone needed a bath. The fire had been lit with wood, then coal had been placed on and it soon burnt to a nice glow. Saucepans would be put on ready for the tin bath which hung on a nail in the outhouse. Gran had put some water ready in the copper and lit the fire underneath it, so we all could have a bath or a wash when the water was hot enough. The tin bath was carried in front of the fire and turns would be taken to get in. The first to get in the bath were the ones with least soot on. Some of us washed in cold water first to get most of the black off, but it didn't really come off that well and it made the towels very dirty.

Facing Castle Mill was a lake which we had heard say many people over the years had committed suicide in, mostly ladies that had been jilted by their young men, or whose young men had been killed in the war. These people would often just leave their shoes on the water's edge for the police to find. It seemed a sad lake to me. Yet plenty of men would go fishing for trout there. The stream that fed the lake was also abundant with fresh water cress. In the field beyond, mushrooms grew as big as saucers. We often went to pick the watercress and mushrooms. One such day there were quite a lot of small branches on the ground, from the high winds the night before. We went back for a sack to collect some for the fire. What a lovely time we were having; everything seemed free. Suddenly we heard the galloping of horses and a man's voice shouting. I held the bag open while Dad and Dolly and Billy put the wood in. We all looked at the galloping Major. That was the name for him; he was the squire of the area, and we were on his land. He said, 'What do you think you are doing?' We told him we were gathering sticks for the fire. We said we were evacuees and lived at Castle Mill.

'Well, empty the sack and clear off,' he said in a very posh voice.

Looking back now I really think he had no right to make us empty the sack out, as we were on a footpath which led from our village to the other.

My aunt had heard from Uncle Jack. He was now in Rangoon in Burma. She had several photos of him taken with the natives and he had told her how he had made friends with a monkey. An American had saved his life. Uncle had been found along the road-side. He had got lost from his regiment. How this letter had got through the censors we never knew. Mostly the forces letters were opened up and read, then sealed and stamped. They were then either posted on or destroyed.

How we loved our Uncle Jack! He often wrote to us, each in turn. Once he sent some lovely photographs of himself. One was of him with this monkey; he was feeding it bananas. Just think of that, in England bananas were so scarce. Uncle Jack looked really suntanned, as though he was on holiday. On another photo he was sitting in a rickshaw, which was like a barrow with a sunshade over the top. It was pulled along by one of the natives. He looked as though he was happy, yet he couldn't wait to get back to England, he wrote.

Back at Castle Mill, life went on. Grandad was really getting too old to go to work. First he had to take a bus about half an hour's ride away. Then he had to work alongside the drayman or hold the horses, rolling the barrels off the cart and down into the cellars of the pubs. So he gave up the work. He said he would like a dog, to be able to take it for a walk. One of the men he had met said that he had a black Labrador bitch which was having pups and they wanted a home for her. Grandad brought her home, much to the delight of everyone.

The day came when she had seven pups, all black with very long tails. Grandad said the tails would have to come off. One Saturday morning we were all at Castle Mill for the day. Two young men came to the door. Gran let them in; they had come to take the dogs' tails off.

'How are you going to do it?' we all said.

'We bite them off!' said one.

What a fuss we all made.

'Well!! We could cut them off.'

And he produced a large knife and grabbed one of the little pups and put him on the kitchen table. How the pup squealed. We were all upset and saying, 'No! No! You can't!'

I really think these two were having a laugh out of us townies. I was to make friends with one of these young men, whose name was Ronald. A few years later I married him. How strange life can be.

CHAPTER 11

The Village Shop

I was to go up to the village every day with Dad while Dolly stayed at Castle Mill. We would go into the village shop to fetch bread and a few cigs for Dad or a half an ounce of Golden Virginia tobacco and a few sweets, if we were lucky enough to have any coupons left. I had already met the postmaster and his wife, Mr and Mrs Amos, and Ada Milner, when we had been up at the farm.

As the shop was a post office it was a hive of activity. This particular day, Mrs Milner asked me if I would like to work for a few hours for her. What a wonderful offer it was: to work in a sweet shop! I was to get one shilling for a morning's work. Just the idea of it was wonderful.

I was shown around the house and shop and large garden and orchard. The house was very old, three or four hundred years, and was made of stone with two-feet thick walls. But they did have electric lights, not gas lamps or candles as the other houses had.

I wasn't shown the counter side of the post office until I had learnt how to serve in the shop. The ration cards and sweet coupons were very difficult to learn to deal with first.

The customers were all local people. They had to register with a shop and then give up their coupons for butter, cheese, lard, sugar, tea and bacon. You could not buy coffee. A few bananas could be had but only the children under five were allowed them. Apples were available as they were local grown. All vegetables were very scarce, so anyone who had a garden would grow their own. This brought back the war effort to me.

Serving in the shop, it was the chatter of war and how London and other cities were being bombed by the Germans.

None of the village people carried their gas masks so I didn't carry mine about any more. Mothers and wives came into the shop-cum-post office to get their weekly allowance which the Army paid out to them. They would pass the book over the counter, and the postmaster would stamp it twice and take out the counterfoil, and put it in a drawer. After closing, he would count up how much he had paid out, and how many stamps, postal orders, money orders, telegrams etc. he had sold and it had to balance out at the end of the week and be sent to the head office in Nottingham.

Mr Milner said he would teach me the post office side later if I stayed with them. Yet I had really come to sell sweets, I thought, and to eat a few, I hoped.

First I had to learn about the ration books and how many coupons to take out of each. All families registered with a shop of their choice. The travelling salesman would come round to see how many were on your books and he would see you had the right amount of groceries and provisions you had coupons for.

I was shown how to cut cheese into two ounce, quarter pound and one pound pieces. They had to be cut from a round, twenty-eight pound piece of cheese with a thick rind on and covered with a tight fitting muslin. It took all my strength to pull it off; also the smell wasn't very nice. The large cheese was first cut in half, then in half again and kept wrapped in white fresh clean muslin at all times.

Lard and margarine came in twenty-eight pound lumps too. That was quite easy to cut up into two, four, six and eight ounces. Lard was a bit greasy especially in warm weather, though that didn't worry Mrs Milner as the back of the shop had the two-foot thick stone walls, which kept the whole place cool. Butter had to be treated in rather a special way. It was delivered by lorry in a wooden barrel with the rest of the items. There were still only two ounces per head a week, so most families had it every other week. But what an effort I had to get the cut just right. Not only was it cut with a knife from out of the barrel, it also had to be patted into a nice oblong shape. No, not with your hands but with two wooden things shaped like spades. It would be put on to greaseproof paper and neatly folded up. Lard and margarine and cheese were all put into greaseproof paper in small parcels. Sugar came in one hundredweight sacks and had to be weighed into half pound and one pound blue strong paper bags, then folded down at the top in a way so they wouldn't come open.

Flour, both self raising and plain, came loose in half hundredweight white sacks: that was fifty-six pounds at a time. All had to be weighed out into strong paper bags. The white flour sacks when empty were washed and boiled in the stone copper and sewn round and crocheted, if you were clever enough to crochet. We would also embroider lovely flower patterns on the white linen flour sacks. They were then tablecloths.

When it came to cutting bacon, that was another story. A whole side of a pig without legs would be brought into the shop and laid across the counter. It was enormous. I thought, how am I going to cut it into rashers? Some people liked their few rashers cut with a knife by hand. But the ribs had to be boned first. Mrs Milner did have a bacon cutter which looked a hundred years old.

The bacon side was called a flitch. It was laid on a metal plate, a handle was turned and the large round wheel cut a slice of bacon. I nearly cut the end of my finger off too the first time I tried it. I did get out of cutting the bacon though, except one day when a bluebottle fly had laid its eggs on the underside of it. There were some fly eggs and some had hatched out and maggots were wriggling all over the unsalted side of the flitch. I was told to fetch the knife and just scrape them off and carry on cutting. After that I always saw that the bacon side was wrapped in a vinegar-smelling muslin. No one knew about the maggots; all the customers had their bacon ration that week. I hoped I had scraped the bacon clean!

There was quite a lot to do in the village shop, though I had hoped it was just selling a few sweets. The other jobs were dusting the shelves every other day and wiping the boxes and jars and tins. Once a week the window had to be emptied of the display items and the small window panes had to be cleaned; that was my job too, it seemed. The lady shop owner had the nice job of putting the adverts made of cardboard back again. Before the war the window would have been piled high with tins of soup, tarantella tomato tins, tins of fruit and packets of Nice biscuits or chocolates that were then in plentiful supply.

Outside windows had to be cleaned as well. When the sun was out there were four hooks to hang a canvas blind on.

I was only working a few hours a day and I went back each day to where Mum and Dad were billeted, which was only few cottages away.

CHAPTER 12

No Silk Stockings

It was now 1942 or 43. Mum and Dad kept saying they wanted to go back to London. Gran and Grandad, Auntie and the children were quite happy in their Castle Mill cottage at Papplewick, even though they would have liked to go back to London.

The American GIs came to England, also Canadians. That was 1942. A lot of the local girls would make dates with the Americans. They had nice smart uniforms and plenty of money and a way with words that the girls fell for. The Canadians didn't have the same smart uniforms or the money to throw about like the GIs.

As I have said, they were very popular. They even had affairs with married young women whose husbands were away fighting. The GIs would bring nylon stockings, cigarettes and chewing gum. They would give them away to whoever was friendly to them. You couldn't blame the girls really because we had never seen nylon stockings here. There were only cotton, what were called lisle, stockings. Silk, of course, was available if you were very rich to buy them.

Most of the girls I knew, in the summer would get some builder's sand and mix it with a little water, then would spread it all over their legs where it would dry a nice tan colour. The rough sand would soon brush off their legs. Another possibility was after the teapot had had cups of tea taken out, to rub the tea leaves on our legs. But that wasn't very successful, because the tea was rationed to only 2 oz a week each person, so there weren't enough tea leaves. Some people who grew their own vegetables would use onion skins. If the skin of the onion was left in water for a

68

while the dark brown water could be dubbed on the legs and left to dry.

Coffee mixed with water would have been perfect but there was no coffee to be had at all in England. Perhaps the Yanks would be able to get some. The Americans were coffee drinkers; the English only drank tea.

Quite a lot of the girls were to marry the Americans and Canadians and when the war was over, they went to live in their husbands' home town. It caused quite an upset with their parents when they went. One of these brides was Ivy, whose mother and father along with her two brothers had been killed. She was my cousin on my mother's side. She came to live for a while with Mum and Dad and Bill at Downham while I was away still at Papplewick, although I did go back and forth to home.

Ivy had married a Canadian, named John. They had two sons born in England and three more children when they went to Canada. During 1943, some years later, John would often bring several of his pals to stay. They would put cushions on the floor to lie on or bring an Army bed roll. Mum and Dad were happy with this as the Canadian boys brought them grey Army blankets, cigarettes, chocolate, even some coffee.

By 1943 Mum and Dad were in London to see how our house was after the air raids. Living on the outskirts of London, in a way we were lucky as we had missed the endless bombing, night after night, by the Germans. They were having the Canadians stay over. Our house was in fairly good condition, though Dad couldn't open the doors and we had to get help with a neighbour to crowbar them open. Some of the windows were smashed but the tape which was criss-crossed over them had saved the glass from falling out. The roof tiles were loose in places where the shrapnel from the English Army big guns had rained down.

Yet the house side was intact, just plenty of dust about and soot down the chimney. The whole house must have shuddered with the bombardments.

We were back again into the very strong black-out procedure. We all still had to get ready any time to go into the Anderson shelter in the back garden. While we were away the inside had kept dry, though Dad said he expected it to be full of water. The sirens still sounded two or three times a day or night. What a contrast to the Midland countryside we had left.

Next door to us, I had two friends; one was working in a bank in London; one was still at school. By staying at home and not being evacuated they had finished or were finishing their education, which I hadn't had, except for a few odd hours in the early part of the war.

The girls next door were soon to put me in the picture of what was happening. They said they would take me dancing to the local Army drill hall. Dad wasn't very happy with that; he didn't think me old enough. He wanted me to join a tennis club and get to know better-off boys and girls. But I wasn't into tennis – or boys, come to that. I think Dad was afraid I would get in with the Canadian young men who came to stay, as some girls seemed to have done.

The girls next door seemed to have done everything I hadn't done. I suppose they were being friendly to me. They said if I was short of clothes such as undies they would tell me where to buy pieces of parachute. These were Army or Air Force parachutes that hadn't been sewn up properly, so people could buy a section for two or three shillings. I had a lovely time cutting and sewing. The nylon material was a dirty colour white, but I was able to buy dyes from the chemist for one or two pennies. I had a pink dye and I cut out three pairs of knickers and three brassieres. The pink dye made them look very elegant. Sexy would be the word in 1997. I also made a half under-skirt and I was several weeks getting elastic to put through the waist as elastic was scarce. The two girls next door had made a swimsuit but hadn't dyed it. When they pegged it on the line it looked a bit scruffy. I had this idea that if I bought another section of parachute I could make a one piece swimsuit and if I could get some shirring elastic, I would sew patterns on the material with the elastic. Of course I would have to cut the swimsuit out larger so that when the elastic was criss-crossed all over it would look smaller but fit beautifully. I then dyed it green. I was very proud of making these garments as it made our clothing coupons go a bit further. The dye soon washed out of the nylon material, so had to be dyed again. The garments never wore out, but the knickers weren't very comfortable to wear, not like the navy blue school knickers.

Christmas had come and gone again and I was still at home. It was now early 1943. The Government had given out that shoes were to be rationed. How, we thought, could shoes be rationed? We soon got used to it. Everyone was allowed two pairs of shoes a year. Sweets were my worst thing to be rationed, as from 1942 we were allowed 12 oz every four weeks. I really loved chocolate toffee, that was my favourite sweet, I also liked sherbert.

Word would often go round that the greengrocer's had got bananas and oranges in. Bananas were only for under fives; no one minded that at all. Oranges were very precious too, so if people were able, they would go off to the shop which had the supply of oranges. What a queue there would be! Only three or four at a time they would let everyone have, till the boxes ran out. No one seemed to mind queueing up as long as they had a little at the end of the wait.

I still wrote long letters to Gran and also to the postmaster and his wife. They said I could go back any time I wanted and stay with them. I thought about it, but really, I still wasn't able to do what I liked. Dad and Mum were fed up with me lying about all the time; they thought I ought to be out at work. One day we went to Catford, our nearest town, by tram. Woolworth's had a notice up: 'Girls wanted to serve on the counter. Fifteen shillings a week.' Dad said it was a good idea for a start, but I had bigger ideas. Having no leaving school certificate, however, I wouldn't get in a bank like my friend next door. I was now fifteen and a big girl and Mum said, 'You're ready for some work.'

'Not that work,' I said.

No way would I go to Woolworth's.

Mum, Dad and I were falling out now all the time. I kept wanting to go back to Papplewick; the postmaster said he would let me have a go at learning the post office procedure. Mum and Dad gave in and let me go.

Someone made arrangements for me to be picked up by car. Car! Very few had a car. Doctors, bank managers, not even the church parson had them; they all rode bikes everywhere. Yet arrangements had been made from Papplewick for me to go back by car. I found out on the journey back that the owners were wealthy clothing shop owners and they lived in Bromley, Kent, which was only a few miles from Downham. They were taking their elderly aunt back to Papplewick after a holiday in Bromley. Mr Milner the postmaster had made arrangements. My bags were packed and I left home, leaving Bill my brother, Mum and Dad.

CHAPTER 13

Village Life

Getting settled in the four hundred year old cottage was really exciting. I had my own bedroom, with a lovely thick feather mattress and soft feather pillows. There was a wardrobe and a chest of drawers and the thing I thought I had seen the back of: the awful guzzunder, the po or chamber pot. Yet I still had to use one.

We three had a meeting round the breakfast table next morning. They said I had to start as I was to go on. What that meant, I didn't know.

Anyhow, getting up was at five thirty. What a dreadful hour, I kept saying. They didn't listen to me. Then came the list of jobs to be done. Mrs Milner would rake the ashes out of the black grate and brush with black lead once a week to keep the grate black and shiny. I was to take the shovels of grey ash out the back and put them onto a heap in the back garden. Then I was told to put on a big old black apron and with a bucket of cold water, scrubbing brush and a bar of hard green soap, get on my knees and scrub the hearth. Then Mrs Milner put the crunched up newspaper in the fireplace, laid sticks over and lit it with a match. When the sticks were burning up, pieces of coal were placed on the top of each other and left. Then a black kettle was filled with water for breakfast tea.

Mr Milner was already out in the garden. He had over a hundred chickens to feed and clean out and two pigs he was fattening up, one for market and one to keep, if he was able to, as the Government had put a restriction on owning and killing a pig.

We three sat down for breakfast on my first day at the post

office cottage in Papplewick. I was to stay there for the next two years.

Many jobs were to come my way, which looking back I never should have done; my parents would not have approved.

After the scrubbing of the hearth I had to get clean, fresh, cold water with the scrubbing brush and cloth and scrubbing soap. A cheaper soap came out to scrub with. The Sunlight soap was best for rubbing dirty clothes with on washday, as I have already mentioned.

With the second bucket of water the doorsteps had to be scrubbed. One step was the front door and the other was the shop step and shop floor and once a week the whole of the shop was scrubbed through. It fell on me to do all this cleaning. Oh! How I wished I could have been strong minded enough to say 'enough is enough'. A wash and change after that and then I could help in the shop, which was rather nice as I could meet people; they all seemed to want to talk to me. I suppose it was because I had a London accent. Many years later I heard the villagers had felt sorry for me.

My other jobs seemed to be endless. There was no sitting and reading a book, which I would love to have done. The wireless only came on to hear the news broadcast several times a day, which was all doom and gloom. The Germans always seem to be gaining ground. The Japanese had come into the war against us. They were taking prisoners, mostly Yanks but some English, Australians and New Zealanders had very bad times. The Japs were very cruel to prisoners. They made them work like slaves in the heat and only fed them on sloppy soup. They were also whipped on their backs to make them work. Many just fell to the ground. Some who retaliated were placed in a hot hole with a grate or wooden door over the top of the hole and the Japs would urinate over the grate onto the men and the smell and heat was unbearable. Many never made it home after the war.

After listening to the news Mrs Milner would get up from the table after breakfast to bread and jam only. She would say, 'Come on. Work, for the night is coming. The day has just begun.' It would still only be about six thirty then.

Soon the baker would arrive and bring bread that had been

ordered the day before. He would be able to bring a few cakes, which he sold out of very quickly. Sometimes the baker would bring Amos some stale bread; he would sell it to him for his pigs. Amos kept two. One he was allowed to fatten up for himself, and pig meal was allocated by the Government for the other one. After four to six months the pig would be sold to the Government Marketing Board, for sale to the public. The other pig could be kept and fed on scraps of waste and of course this old bread bought from the baker. The scraps were usually potato peelings, carrot, parsnip and swede peelings. All the peelings were boiled up in an old saucepan over the fire, and smelt the house out while they were cooking. It used to make me feel sick. Amos would say, 'You'll get used to it.' I never did.

Mondays were always washday. What a performance it was. The copper was lit as I have mentioned earlier in this book. Water was put on to boil. Whites were all washed with Sunlight soap first, collars and cuffs scrubbed, then put into the copper to boil, then taken out and put into a tin bath to be rinsed. After the rinsing certain pieces such as table cloths, cuffs and collars were put in last for weak starch. Then all had to be put through the wooden mangle. I was left to get the towels out of the copper and rinse them two or three times, a back aching job, while Mrs Milner put the washing on the line, if the weather was fine. So Mondays came and went and in between I served in the shop along with Mr and Mrs Milner.

I had another job lined up for me. It was to take bread and groceries out on a delivery bike. How that basket hung heavy on my arm. There would be six or eight loaves and other items. Some of the rationed food I took by this bike method. The houses I went to were big and fine, owned by the squire from Papplewick Hall, a solicitor, a factory owner and a bank manager. The houses had very long drives. I would cycle as far as I could, then leave the bike and carry this heavy basket of groceries. I was usually lucky to be able to wheel the bike up to the back door. When I first went to one particular large house I went to the first door I came to. It happened to be their front door, and a man in a uniform said,

'Round the back way, girl.'

I said, 'My name is Winnie.'

I then had to pass the barking dogs with the bike and open several gates to get to the back. I thought, if there was a next time I would leave the order on the front doorstep.

I had some greaseproof paper in the basket, to cover the goods over. The man in uniform was a butler in the house. Most of these large houses had servants, a cook or housemaid or butler, and cleaner and gardener.

Every day now I had to take the orders out, wet or fine. I really wasn't very happy with this at all.

One day I went with an order to a house which happened to be a head gardener's house. It was a dark wet day and the gardener said, 'Hello, duck.' Everyone was called duck (pronounced dook!) if they didn't know your name. He said, 'Come in and take your wet things off. Have a warm by the fire.'

I noticed there was no one about, so I declined the offer, although the fire looked inviting. I had many close encounters like this. One other day I was to go on my rounds and take bread, not to the large houses but to the cottages.

I knocked on the door. No one came. I wasn't going to take the bread back after they had ordered it. So I opened the door, back door of course. I had been told by Mr Milner not to use the front doors ever again. Being a Cockney girl, I said to him, 'Well! Why not? I don't want my bum bit off with their big dogs.'

Anyway, I opened the back door on to a porch, and suddenly the door closed with a loud bang. The man of the house stood there.

'How about a kiss, Cockney kid?' he said.

My heart was pounding. I had never been so close to a man before, apart from my Dad. He squashed me against the door. I couldn't move and he put his arms over my shoulders. He tried to kiss me. How I wriggled and shoved him off. He came to his senses when he knew I was not happy with the situation.

I wasn't able to tell anyone about this so I still had to take the bread there, yet it never occurred again.

On another occasion I went to take a loaf of bread to a bungalow. I had put the bread on the table, when the lady of the house said, 'Hello dear!' (Not 'duck' as she was a bit upmarket.) She said, 'Would you like to see my mother?'

I said, 'I don't mind.' I was really a bit daft then.

She took me into the front room to see her mother, who was dead and in her coffin. I really was upset. I couldn't get out of the house quickly enough. I made my way back on the bike; it was the last bread delivery for that day, thank goodness.

Lunch time would be a big dinner. We always had pudding first. If it was Yorkshire pudding you could have gravy on it or jam; then it was followed by potatoes, meat of some kind and brussels sprouts or cabbage, all home grown. Tea would be at 3.30 p.m. and would be brown bread and butter cut so thin you could see the plate pattern through the bread. There was jam or marmalade in the winter on the bread, or home grown cucumber and tomatoes in the summer, maybe watercress which we would gather from the local brook which was fresh running water. There might be cake after or jelly with an apple cut up in it, or apple and sugar and bread and butter, which I grew to like very much.

The jobs were always there, every day and all day. Window cleaning outside, the pavement swept first outside.When it was fruit picking time I had to help get the apples off the trees and they had to be wiped clean, put into flat wooden boxes and kept in a cool place. Pears had to be handled very carefully as they were very ripe. Some of the fruit had to be taken into the shop to be sold. Runner beans and broad beans were picked and sold in the shop.

The potatoes, carrots, onions and beetroots which Mr Milner grew all had to be dug up from the ground and kept away from frost for the winter. The out-houses of the cottage were very cool, the walls all being two feet thick.

On the side of the cottage ran a long out-house which Mr Milner told me had been a school for the Papplewick children. There had only been twenty-one attending as they had to pay a halfpenny a week to learn. There were two very old wooden desks; he said they were over one hundred years old and that was in 1943. He also showed me an ink well made out of stone and a feather quill pen which he thought the teacher would have used.

There were old hooks in rows which had been hand-made by a blacksmith. Perhaps it was his father, who was the local blacksmith, who had had them made. Mr Milner had been a blacksmith at Linby pit for twenty-three years before becoming the local postmaster. The old iron hooks would have had the children's coats and hats on. I could almost imagine a cane hanging there, ready to give the children a disciplinary whack if they were late or cheeky. The teacher would whack them on their hands several times, or across their bottom. There were slates that had been used for writing on with a slate pencil. This was used instead of books.

Mr Milner said that when he was younger he could remember a well full of water being filled up in the yard next door and most of the items from the old school had been thrown down it. I believe it must have been the smallest school in England. To me it was only like a passageway.

CHAPTER 14

Summer 1943

Mr Milner would rear his own chicks in incubators. The eggs would be put into the box which had a paraffin lamp on all the time. I helped Mr Milner put them in. They had to be turned over every day for twenty-one days. It was really so exciting when the day came and the chicks were cracking open the eggs and slowly getting out of their shells. Some would die, but most would be soon running and chirping, looking for food, a few hours after they came out of the shell. It was a wonderful sight to see them.

The chicks were still kept warm with a paraffin lamp until a week later when they would be allowed to be moved to a larger but still small house, where they would run in and out. Mr Milner said, 'I am going to have an electric incubator one of these days.' He never did.

The chicks grew quite quickly; he said we would have some pullet eggs in about six months.

'Pullet eggs? whatever are they?' I said.

He replied, 'The first eggs laid by a young chicken.'

It was lovely, I thought. Not about Christmas time, it wasn't, when I had to help get a few older hens ready for the dinner table.

One particular day, Mr Milner said to me, 'Come up the garden to see which hen we shall kill first.'

I went up the garden later than I should have done. Several birds were upside down, tied by their feet, hung on the branch of an apple tree. They were still wriggling and flapping their wings, but Mr Milner assured me they were dead. He had one more hen to kill. He put the bird in between his knees and twisted its head round and round. I was in a state at seeing this and shouted at him to stop. He was startled by me and he let the hen get away,

What an awful sight I saw then; the hen ran round and round the garden with its head hanging down. Blood was coming out of its mouth, and the noise it made was blood-curdling. Mr Milner chased it and swore at it or me, I didn't know which. He was able to catch up with it and put it out of its misery. I was told some hens had their heads chopped off and were then hung up by their legs so the blood ran out of their bodies.

The next job I had was to help with plucking out the feathers. There was a very old shallow brown sink inside the scullery. I had to put one of the birds in the sink, hold it with one hand and pull feathers out with the other. Mr Milner would say, 'Mind you don't tear the skin. I won't be able to get a good price if the skin is torn.'

I really didn't know what he meant at first, but after plucking four or five I soon got to understand why they had to look perfect. Mind you, after the plucking was the next horrible job. It was to get the inside cleaned out. With a pair of old scissors and a sharp knife, the head had to be cut off (unless of course it had been chopped off to kill the poor hen). With the scissors and my hand covered in blood and fine feathers I was shown how to snip the neck down so its windpipe and craw could be pulled out quite easily. The craw is where its food would go into before going into its intestines. There was very little smell or mess with this end. The bottom end was worse until I got used to cleaning them. First a small cut was made in the skin at the rear end and I had to put my hand up its bottom to draw out the insides. It was a messy, smelly job which I hated. There were yards of tubes of skin with mess in and attached to that were smaller tubes of skin with eggs from the size of pin heads to almost normal large eggs with soft shells. The pin-head size eggs were all joined together in one mass. It seemed a shame to have wrung these poor hens' necks to be eaten for dinner when they had so many days and weeks left to go on laying. I asked why they had to be sold for eating and the reply was that the eggs were being laid with soft shells. The feet were cut off last and after all the innards were taken out the bird would be run under a cold tap for a good wash. That might sound a simple thing to do, but how very cold the water was on my hands. It was as cold as ice as it had been pumped up from a well below the ground. All the feathers were gathered up and sometimes the clean ones were saved to make cushions. I had the job of cleaning the feathers; heads, feet and insides were thrown away. What a messy job for one so young, I thought.

Mrs Milner would wipe the chickens dry and tie up the legs and wings with fine string, then weigh them and cover them with greaseproof paper and put a price on each. But I still had not finished with the hens as when they were ordered they had to be delivered to the houses who wanted them.

The weekly orders were made up with the rations all allocated, and the bread, to be delivered along with the oven-ready chickens. On one occasion a lady had ordered three chickens with just their necks wrung and their feet tied together. These were placed on the handle bars of the bicycle and so as I rode along the road the blood from the heads was splashing on my shoes and on the road. How did I get into this situation?

I was to get to know most of the village people. Some were nice, but some were a bit queer. Once I heard a noise outside the bedroom window, but the next morning I said to myself I must have dreamt about the noise. Looking down, however, I could see several men and Mr Milner shouting and waving their arms about, A herd of cows had got in the garden in the night and what a mess they had made. Their feet had trampled on everything, all the plants and vegetables. The garden smelt too, with urine and cow pats everywhere; even the hedges were splattered with cow muck. Mr Milner said he would see if the farmer would get some men in to wash the paths and hedges clean. I kept my fingers crossed and hoped I wouldn't have to help.

One particular morning I was making the bed and emptying the guzzunder, and on looking out of the window in the yard next door I could hear a lot of squealing. It sounded like a pig. It was being pushed with a stick into the yard. There were a few buckets and a bath about, with two or three men and a very large knife. I stood looking down and I couldn't move; I was petrified; the pig was squealing in a terrible way when one of the men stuck the knife in the pig's neck under its mouth. The blood spurted out, then one of the men with his coat off and his sleeves rolled up to above his elbow put his arm in the slit under the pigs jaw. 'Why?' I asked later. I was told it was to get the squeal out. I didn't believe that story. The pig went on squealing and rolling about for what seemed like hours: I was told it was about half an hour. I ran down the stairs and was crying and shouting how cruel they were. I vowed never to eat pork again, and I never did for many years.

They had a lovely dog at this post office billet. I would put a hat on him and a skirt and he would stand on two legs and dance with me. I would then sit him down and Mr and Mrs Milner would be my audience. I would hitch my dress skirt up to the top of my legs and put a bow in my hair and sing a Shirley Temple song, then put a scarf on my head and sing some of the old London songs. They were sung all over the country yet I thought they were only for Londoners. They were songs such as 'Knees up Mother Brown' and 'Show me the way to go home' which was my favourite; and 'Bye bye Blackbird'. Then I would go on to sing some of the current war songs, like, 'There'll be Blue Birds over the White Cliffs of Dover'.

They seemed to like my singing. I would lie in my bedroom and sing myself to sleep, Mr and Mrs Milner as well. They did invite me to sleep and sing in between them in their bed, but I never accepted that kind of offer.

Briny the dog was my best friend. I would take him for a walk, when the shop closed, for a run in the meadow. Mr Milner would say, 'While you're there, look for some watercress in the stream that runs at the bottom of the meadow. Pick plenty. Then some can be sold in the shop tomorrow.'

He might have been making fun of me but I did bring some back if it was there to pick.

The day came when I couldn't find Briny. I was so distressed. I went in the garden and looked in the pig sty, where the pigs were being fattened up to be sold. He wasn't there.

Up I went to the top where the chickens were. No Briny. I then went into the top field. 'Briny, Briny,' I called. Still no Briny. I wandered down to the house looking behind everything and finally asked Mr Milner, 'Where is Briny?'

He couldn't say. Even Mrs Milner wouldn't or couldn't say.

82

Really I should've gone home then but I had no money and Mum and Dad hadn't been in touch with me lately. I really felt like little orphan Annie.

The days and the weeks went past and I never ever got to know where my doggy friend Briny went to. Mr and Mrs Milner didn't seem at all upset by Briny not being there, which was a puzzle to me as he was their dog. Perhaps the country people weren't as soft as us townies.

The war still seemed a long way off. Locals would come in the post office and shop for a few cigarettes and matches and would stand and have a few words. They would tell us where their husbands were fighting, if they knew.

One or two local boys had been taken prisoner. Quite a lot had gone off to war in the village.

I heard, as I was taking bread out to a couple of houses, that on the doorstep of one of them, as the housewife opened the front door she saw a strange thing. She told me how she bent to have a closer look at what someone had left on the doorstep. It was a hard boiled egg which had been peeled of its shell and a coloured feather was stuck in the top. I had to have a little laugh but this lady said, 'Don't laugh as I have had several things left on my doorstep over the past few months.'

Most of the items were hard boiled eggs. These were on ration, but a few people would have an odd hen or two for eggs. One time there was an egg and it had a chalk ring drawn round with the words on her step saying, 'You're next.'

I didn't laugh any more as it was quite serious. As the weeks went past the boiled eggs stopped being put on my friend's doorstep and a dead mouse or bird was left instead. I think she had an idea who it was doing this, otherwise she would have informed the police. It was really like witchcraft being performed on her. Nothing more was said or done.

I was still doing the rounds, taking the bread out daily on the bike with the large basket full of groceries. How it hurt my arm to carry it even a short distance from the bike to the door, as I have said before.

I would go to several large houses in the village and always had to make the deliveries round the back. On this particular day it was quite early, eight o'clock-ish. I knocked on the back door and a tiny little girl, so thin with a pale face and ginger hair, opened it. She only looked about ten or eleven, yet she must have been fourteen to be working, although I had been working much younger.

She was in the middle of scrubbing the large stone-slabbed kitchen floor and couldn't stop to take the bread from me because the missus of the house was a strong minded battle-axe of a woman. She used her tongue like a whip; she was a very harsh speaking woman. Everyone would jump to her command. There were several small girls who worked at this house. They must have been chosen to work there because of their stature, the lady of the house being so large and dominating. In fact they were all large, the whole family.

The poor little thin girls had to carry buckets of coal up to the first floor after cleaning out the fireplaces, then light the fires in four or five rooms. I had felt sorry for myself until I had met these girls. They all had to live in so we had something in common, being away from home.

As time went by I quite liked the village and the local people, The work at the post office, I did get used to, though I had no time off. If there was any time to spare Mr and Mrs Milner would soon find a job for me.

What I had never done before was painting and decorating. The decorating was called Walpurmuring (emulsioning today). The curtains were taken down, washed and ironed. Hand made rugs were taken out onto the line and beaten till all the dust was out. Furniture was covered over with either newspaper or old sheets. With one of Mr Milner's old shirts on and a scarf round my hair. I would be told to 'slap dab' the ceiling. The walls were white, pink or yellow. I did like doing this after a while, it just didn't seem a real job to do. The lino had to be washed over and the furniture put back, also the curtains hung along with the beaten rugs. I was really worn out as I felt I was doing it all, as Mrs Milner was in the shop and couldn't leave it. Mr Milner was always busy with his hens and two pigs or the vegetables needed watering or weeding.

CHAPTER 15

Passing of the Years

The months were passing, even the years. A war was on, but no one in the village seemed bothered except the few upset families whose husbands and sons were away fighting.

At the village institute or hall there would be various people having bazaars, the proceeds going to good causes such as the Red Cross or Barnardo's Homes for orphans. Most of the villagers would knit or sew things. Some would give garden produce; some women would make cakes. There were table top games of 'roll the pennies', 'Hoop La' or 'Guess how many dried peas in a pot'. There were small prizes. The aim was to get as much money as possible for the special causes.

Mrs Milner had a great idea for me to do. It was to hold a dance in the institute. I chose to send all the proceeds to Dr Barnardo's. Though I say it myself, it was quite a feat to arrange. The hall had to be booked and some sort of music. In the small town of Hucknall were several 'one man bands' who would have a gramophone and a set of two or three drums, with some kind of trumpet and castanets as well. The one I chose always played the sounds of the dance music of Victor Sylvester. There was an MC whose full title was Master of Ceremonies who would announce each dance. It was all very professionally done.

The half time refreshments were a huge success. Every item had been donated by the villagers. One very kind lady had made me two large cakes; one was a chocolate cake with cream inside and the other was plain with vanilla cream. The cakes were much bigger than dinner plates and would cut up into twenty-four pieces each. Other ladies made scones or queen cakes. I did wonder how they got the sugar and the butter and eggs to make them. Perhaps they were able to buy extras on the black market.

Most shops did get extras and would let a few customers have them, charging higher prices; this was called buying on the 'black market'.

The dances were wonderful. Several people from other villages would come and pay sixpence to come into the hall and would dance the night away. The MC would come over to me and teach me how to dance. There would be an odd soldier or two on leave and several young men.

These young men had to register at eighteen and if the number on the card they were given was 'O', those young men had to go in the mines. They were given the name of 'Bevan Boys' after the Employment Minister of this time. The rest of the boys were also made to do what was required. Some went into the Army while others went on the land.

These young men who worked in the mines had good wages and would have a good time, as they called it. They would all meet up in the local pubs or the Gaiety dance hall in Hucknall. At this time the young Polish Air Force men were stationed in the area. It was a regular place for fights to go on between them The road would be covered with broken bottles and patches of blood. Hundreds of girls went out with the Poles and ended up marrying them. Over the years they made very good husbands and bought houses and settled down locally.

I was able to arrange a dance at the Papplewick village hall once a month. Everyone looked forward to them. All proceeds I sent off to different charities.

At one of these social events one of my friends brought her two brothers who worked on their father's farm. My cousin Dolly would dance with the eldest whose name was Alex. He was quite taken up with her: who wouldn't be, with her black curly hair, big brown eyes, white teeth and pink and white skin. Why he was smitten was because she wore red for the dances. He would call her his 'little poppy'. There was a song 'Amapola my pretty little poppy' which everyone knew and sang around 1943 or 44.

The younger brother, aged about twenty, came to take me out. Taking out, in the war years, would be going to the pictures, but I didn't go with him as he didn't have any money from his father's farm, only the privilege to work there. We went on the odd walk or two and I was invited to the farm for tea, to see my friend Irene as well. They made me very welcome and would ask questions all the time about bombing and the evacuation from London. I do believe they just wanted to listen to how I spoke, coming as I did from the south.

Time came for me to go back to the post office. I would not have to be late as they were very old fashioned.

The social dances were really wonderful for the village. I was rather pleased with myself to think I was doing all the arranging.

On another Saturday dance a young good looking man came through the door. He found a seat next to one of the nannies who worked in the village; she was fifteen or sixteen – we were all about the same age. They seemed to get on well, I hoped he would look at me, but no. I went over to them and said, 'What about you dancing and in the interval buy some tea and cakes.'

I just wanted to get a closer look at this young man really. He never asked me to dance, ever.

I went home to my post office billet with Alex, my cousin Dolly, and Harry, the younger brother of Alex. We were nearly outside where I lived when Harry pulled me to him and kissed me. From nowhere there was such a commotion. My handsome young man had followed us with Beth the nanny. She only lived two houses away from me, that's why they were just behind us.

Suddenly, Harry was knocked on the floor with one punch and Alex had a front tooth knocked out. It was all because I had resisted Harry's goodnight kisses. It was all over in a few moments. I went into my lodgings and nothing was heard of it again.

I did go for a walk with Harry again, much to my regret. We walked through the woods which were joined to his farm. I had had to see his sister to say farewell as she was going into the Navy, and Harry walked me home. I had to be back early after lunch to get a few more chores done at the post office before tea, after which I went to Evensong at either Papplewick or Linby church. The church would be full in the 1940s, with everyone praying for their loved ones to come home safe and sound. Most prayed for the war to end.

As I walked back to Papplewick we had to pass a wood. Harry suddenly said, 'Come on, let's go and look.' I could hear noises like the sound of someone treading on twigs and small branches that had broken off. I looked round. I thought it was the ghost lady of the lake coming out of the water nearby, or perhaps one of the ghosts Mr Tillson had told me about when we were up at the farm. Suddenly, Harry put an arm round me and pushed me against a tree. What he was trying to do did not interest me and I broke free of him, ran onto the path and into a herd of cows. I was even more scared of these huge beasts than the one I had just got away from.

CHAPTER 16

Boy Scouts and Cubs

Sunday, after the church service, was a good time for local people to pass the time of day with each other. I came out of the church with some of the Scouts and Cubs and one of the Scout leaders started to say, 'If anyone would like to give a hand on Wednesday nights with the young ones?'

I said, 'I'd like to, if Mr and Mrs Milner would let me.' I was rather surprised they said yes, as they were responsible for me. It was amazing they agreed. Through that time from 1941 till a few years later I stayed in their care.

Every Wednesday evening was rather enjoyable. I walked through the meadow over the bridge into the next village and into the school where the Cubs were attending. I was shown by the leader of the Scouts what to do and how to tie knots and make a camp fire, and I learnt the lovely songs which were sung by everyone. I had a uniform of brown and beige coloured skirt and blouse and a lovely big felt hat and scarf and woggle. How proud I was to wear this.

Once a month at eleven a.m. we would all have to assemble in the school and march in file to church for the service.

1944 was a year when everything was happening. The war was still raging, even though D-Day had taken place in 1944. Most men had been called up by this year. Quite a number of girls went into the munitions and the Land Army. I was just that bit too young to do any of these heroic things.

I'd had a few lessons in how to run a post office. I knew now it wasn't just selling stamps. I had been invited to go to work in a large office about four miles away in Arnold, but it was a difficult place to get to. I had to ride Mrs Milner's sit-and-beg bike that was so old fashioned and cycle about two miles, where arrangements had been made for me to leave it at a house nearby. Then I had to cross over the road to catch a bus into Arnold and walk for about ten minutes to the office.

My first day was rather awe inspiring. There were five people behind the counter but I was shown to an empty drawer and counter and given fifty pounds in notes and change and a ledger book, to make the sales balance. The queue in front of me was endless. The others behind the counter were just as busy. Life went on for about four weeks; the postmaster was okay and we all had to do turns of sending telegraph messages over the phone. That was fine, until it was my turn to learn the telephone operator's job, which was awful. You had to sit in front of a board with bells ringing at you all the time; you had to answer and plug the people on the end of the phone into whichever number they required. I was totally unable to do this kind of work, for what reason I don't know. This was part of the job, so, I had to leave. But it served me in good stead for the years ahead, if only for the counter side.

I was glad to get out of going to Arnold as the journey back to the village in the winter days were a nightmare. In all weathers I'd wait for a bus, knowing that at the end, I had to bike ride in the wet and wind. I did get paid for the weekly work, and was able to keep the money and so send Mum and Dad a ten shilling note in their weekly letter. That had to stop, though, when the Arnold job finished.

Mrs Milner started to pay me ten shillings a week, which was very nice, though I only sent ten shillings home now and again.

One particular day I had gone outside the cottage to fill the coal bucket for the evening. I had to struggle to carry it to the fireplace as it was very heavy.

Sitting round the table were two men who were sitting with some papers in their hand talking to Mr Milner. He looked a little unhappy. One said to me, 'Would you mind answering a few questions?'

I couldn't really say no.

He said, 'We have reason to believe you have been handling and passing over tea coupons.'

More tea was coming into the shop than the amount of tea coupons that were collected off the customers. I said I wouldn't do such a thing, but I was a suspect. I suppose that Mr and Mrs Milner had got some on the black market and had sold it to the rich people of the village. Nothing more was heard of this incident, however, until some time later when we heard it was one of the salesmen who had been fiddling the coupons, so we were all in the clear, thank goodness.

CHAPTER 17

V1s and V2s

I had a break and went home. I would go on the train from Nottingham to St Pancras in London. Sometimes it took five or six hours, standing all the way. The trains were always packed with the forces going with their kit bags, which filled the train up.

I had been up to the library and had heard that southern England and the home counties had had another call from the enemy. It was in June 1944 when the buzz-bombs started. You really didn't know where these were going to drop. These V1 pilotless planes had an explosive on board. We called them doodlebugs or buzz-bombs. While you could hear the engine overhead you felt you were safe. We had all thought that now the planes had stopped bombing our towns and cities we would have peace at last. Yet that was not to be. The Germans never gave up trying to wear us down so southern England and London had these V1 doodlebugs coming over, and when they dropped out of the skies they shattered buildings and killed many people, though our gunners on the coasts with their anti aircraft guns were able to shoot some of them down before they got to the main southern towns.

Worse was to come. The Germans had another more powerful machine which was developed a few months later, called a V2 rocket. There was no defence from this monster. It carried more explosives than the V1 and it was deadly. It made no sound in the sky, but just dropped down. My experience was a bad one for me, but much worse for those which the V2 dropped on.

I had been out shopping and there was this terrible explosion. I recall people running about screaming and shouting. I had a lucky escape even though I had been thrown under a hedge and a wooden shed door was over the top of me. It had been blown out by the blast and had landed on me. I could hear someone saying, 'Are you all right?'

I could hardly talk as I was so frightened and I was breathing in dust as well. I was picked up by one of the air raid wardens. What a jolly man he was. He said, 'Pick yourself up, brush yourself down and start all over again.'

I really was to remember his saying in the years ahead. I did have to report to the doctors for a check up, but I had a good report. Mum was very upset by my experience.

Over in France we heard on the wireless that Britons and Americans and Canadians were really pushing the Germans back, and they were retreating. I was back again in Papplewick. I wasn't very happy at home with Mum and Dad entertaining the soldiers though they were all very well mannered. I had my own room at Mr and Mrs Milner's and they were happy to have me. I was a good help to them.

Bath time at the Milners was the worst thing for me, and using the outside loo. The loo was halfway up the garden with a large bucket and a wooden seat for one. The usual cut up pieces of newspaper were on a nail at the side.

Water was a problem at bath time unless it was Monday night after washday, when the copper fire would be kept in to heat some water then ladled out into a bucket and carried to the bath. I suppose I was lucky it wasn't a tin bath in front of the parlour fire as it had been a few years before. Mr Milner had had a big cast iron bath put in one of the small rooms next to the kitchen. There was no heating in the room, so the hot water was carried to the bath and poured in. We weren't allowed to put in any bath oil, only soda which we sold in the shop in boxes for 1¹/₂d. for one pound. It was wonderful, like white coloured pieces of rock. It was used for softening water for the bath or for washing up and doing the washing. Mr Milner was rather old fashioned yet kind.

If we had a bath any other day, the water would be from a cast iron box at the side of the fire which was made of black cast iron. There would be very little water for a bath from this, possibly two gallons, yet we all managed quite well.

One day I felt I had the itches in my head. How I scratched and scratched. I thought I ought to comb my hair. The shop sold fine-tooth combs that were double sided and I had one of these with newspaper on my knee and combed through my hair.

Oh! What a terrible sight I saw! On the paper after combing through my hair there were the biggest fleas you ever saw. I had to press them with another comb to kill them. They were running all over the newspaper. I had to tell Mrs Milner but I was out of my mind how to. I felt sure she would throw me out.

Yet she was quite calm about it. She washed my hair in hot water with a handful of soda and the other thing she used I hated for ever. It was a spoonful of paraffin. Paraffin is an oil which was used for everything. One such use was to soak a rag in paraffin and wipe all garden tools after they were used. It was used for softening paint brushes. Mostly it was used for lighting lamps to read or see with but we used a little for my hair. I had to wash my hair every day for a week, and it did clear it up. All these things were happening to me, so I felt I wanted to go home.

CHAPTER 18

Apple Picking Again

There were lovely times picking Bramley apples from the back garden, also Newton's Wonder and Keswicks. These had to be sorted and the best sold to the privileged few in the village. Beans had to be picked and sold. Blackberries too were sold in the shop, and tomatoes from the two greenhouses. This was a lovely job. The shop and post office was like a beehive with people in all the time. No wonder Mr and Mrs Milner wanted me to help. Everyone knew each other and tales were told over the counter.

Word had got round the village that a Huntley and Palmer biscuit lorry had parked outside the shop. The villagers came from all over the village to see if they could get half a pound of biscuits. They came in seven pound square tins all packed tightly. There were wafer and cream ones, shortcake and custard creams, but there were only three tins.

Whenever I went to serve I would sneak one. I couldn't resist them as it was about nearly four years since nice things were to be had.

I opened one of the custard cream biscuit tins and to my horror they were mostly broken. Someone had dropped them. No! No! Not me! I knew I hadn't. How could I tell Mrs Milner? But I had to as I was the first to open them. She was horrified and said, 'How clumsy could you be?'

I thought she could sell them as broken biscuits. The customers would be glad to get any. It was days before they spoke to me and I would do the same chores sweeping outside the shop at 5.30 in the morning, scrubbing the doorstep then the shop. I would have bread and butter or porridge for breakfast not both. By the second day I was getting really fed up with all the work and not speaking, over something I hadn't done. Why did I get the blame for things? I don't know. We three sat round the breakfast table and I blurted out, 'I'm going to see the billeting officer to find me another home.'

That made them sit up. The billeting officer was a lady of high standard in the village and one of their best customers. They decided to phone Huntley and Palmer to replace the biscuits, but they wouldn't or couldn't do that. They would perhaps get a refund of some kind for the broken ones. This they did get eventually and all the biscuits got sold.

They were lucky to have a phone. One reason was because it was a shop and post office; people with businesses, also well off folk, all had phones.

Life was getting a little better for me by now. Mrs Milner was making me a grey flannel two-piece suit. I had to make a blouse. I hadn't done anything like it before.

There was a lovely large shop in Hucknall that sold dress material and patterns and knitting wools, socks, dresses and coats. I fell in love with this piece of pink lace, just big enough for a blouse. I was allowed to choose the buttons. It was like looking at jewels in Aladdin's cave, I'd read about in books. I chose seven round mother of pearl buttons. I was so lucky as Mrs Milner also bought me a pair of black shoes. I was in heaven. She was a nice lady.

We got the suit and blouse finished for the Harvest Festival and Papplewick church was full of all the local villagers. I felt so proud to be dressed in a tailored grey suit; it was tailored as Mrs Milner had been a tailoress by trade, working for a small shop in Hucknall which had made most of the suits for men and women who lived in the area. Mrs Milner, she really loved me, her little evacuee. From that day forth, when I wrote to them years after, I would always sign off,

'From your little evacuee.'

1944 was nearly coming to an end. Our fighters and bombers had set about blasting the bases of the V1s and V2s.

The Home Guard were the men who would have acted as soldiers if the Germans had invaded us, though they wouldn't have stood a chance with the might of the enemy in the early part of the war. The Home Guard was disbanded together with quite a lot of other restrictions. The blackout that was the dark curtains and black paper blinds would soon be put out of the way for ever, we hoped. Those that had cars or lorries could take the sticky paper from their lights. All around the coast, though, I was told had to keep the war time restrictions just in case of an enemy invasion. We all still were on rations: the war wasn't over.

Mr Milner said it would be good for me, in the September of 1944, to join the night school in Hucknall. Life was much easier now. So one evening they both went on the bus with me to enrol me. I was persuaded to do a business course, also French. The books for the maths were a bit beyond me as I had only had less than one month schooling of any kind in the years from 1939 till 1944. I came away with no diploma, but a report on being 'a good trier'.

Christmas of 1944 was much happier for most people except those whose loved ones were fighting in Europe and Russia; the Japanese were also a terrible menace. Uncle Jack hadn't come back from Rangoon. His family had had a letter from the Army to say he had been injured. But not by the Japs, the enemies. He had been found lying on the roadside on his own. An American soldier found him unconscious with bruises all over him. Most of the British Army hated the Yanks, but this rescuer was different. The English boys were only jealous of them; they didn't really hate them. The Americans had more Army pay, and their Army uniforms were made of better cloth and therefore smarter looking. Most girls adored them.

Poor Uncle never came home from the Army before the war ended. After a few weeks in sick bay he was ready to handle a gun with a bayonet. He, with his unit, was sent to Colombo, in Ceylon.

A few weeks before Christmas 1944 I was busy arranging another dance. There was the village institute to be booked, and a two-man band with a drum, accordion and records. Tickets were sold or people could pay on the door. Food had to be acquired, which was quite an effort with the rationing on. The villagers were very good to me if I asked if they could spare or make cakes. They would bring baskets of biscuits, cakes and sandwiches.

Mrs Milner gave me the tea to put in the urn. I wonder how she was able to give me tea that was rationed. I had lots of help.

Some lent small Christmas trees and put paper garlands up for me. The wooden floor needed some french chalk to make the dancers glide around. The chemist usually supplied french chalk, which was like talcum powder, but Mrs Milner came up with some from under her counter, which had been put there along with tins of crab and salmon and fruit. They were all like gold dust, yet they were piled up there and a few of the VIPs of Papplewick had some for Christmas and Easter.

I had almost forgotten; I really must get some more posters designed and put up in the village and other places, so I had to look out for my handsome young man who had hand printed some before for me. The proceeds from the dance were going to the Red Cross this time.

Mr Milner said I could have some holly to get a bit of festivity to the hall. The snow had come early that year and in the top field where the holly bushes were, snow was almost eighteen inches thick. I put Mr Milner's large wellingtons on and armed myself with a pair of old scissors which must have been as old as the house, about three hundred years, they were so rusty. I did get some lovely pieces with red berries on too. The country folk say if there are lots of berries on the hedges, it will be a hard winter, which was proving true to their old wives' tales. I had started to cut a piece when I was disturbed by a bird, black and white; it was a magpie. I had learnt a little about the country with being evacuated. The magpie really gave me a fright. He hopped on top of the snow covered hedge and appeared to be talking, as magpies often do. It sounded as though he was saying, 'What are you doing? What are you doing?' He was flapping about and squawking and I couldn't get down the path, which was covered in a hard pounded snow, quickly enough.

Mr Milner wondered what all the fuss was about. He went out after I had taken his wellingtons off to see if he could see this magpie. He really thought I was making a bit of a fuss over a bird.

Several days later, we had another fall of snow overnight. I went with Mr Milner to feed his hens which had to be kept penned up in their shed as the snow was too deep. Mr Milner had his shovel ready to clear some of the snow away from the door of his hen house. When the black and white bird flew straight at him and was flitting and flapping and hopping in front of him, he swung the shovel at it. Good job it missed. I really thought the magpie flew off laughing.

As the days went by Christmas was in most people's thoughts. In mine was still the arrangements for the dance at the village hall. We almost forgot about the bird.

Mum said I should go back home but I was quite happy, though busy and doing a lot of jobs I really didn't feel I should be doing.

The winter of 1944 passed by; the snow never cleared till February 1945. The village Christmas dance was a great success. I had eighty-four pounds to send to the Red Cross. I had a lovely reply from the head office to thank me and all who helped.

Early 1945 was quite eventful. Night school started again. This time I was to take the book-keeping course plus typing and shorthand, which I rather liked, though the book-keeping was a better subject for me. The Thursday nights were for typing and shorthand. I had a distraction outside when I came out. If I missed the bus it was a good half hour walk home back to my billet. I was coming out of the night school and coming out too was my handsome young man, Ronald. He would walk me back to Papplewick pushing his cycle, then rode home after seeing me in to Mrs Milner.

We would walk and talk and we found ourselves fond of each other. We would only hold hands walking, and a fleeting kiss goodnight was so sweet it was unbearable. The same went on for several months. Mr and Mrs Milner knew nothing of our friendship as I wouldn't dare stay out late, not for five minutes.

CHAPTER 19

Valentine's Day

I had to help move one of the hen houses; it was only a small one. We had had some warmer days by February; the snow had turned to rain and the old country saying is, 'February fill dyke, black or white,' meaning it could snow a lot or rain a lot which would clear away the snow.

The 14 February was St Valentine's Day and pushed under the shop door were seven cards, mostly hand made. Mrs Milner brought them in after breakfast and handed them to me.

She said, 'You're very popular.'

I said, 'Who could they be from?'

With Valentine cards most people put a fictitious name on unless of course they were from your true love. I had everyone's name on except any boy I knew, so I just didn't make any comment about the cards. Mr and Mrs Milner had fun guessing.

A few days later the cards had been forgotten. I suppose they were from some of the farm labourers who were having fun sending them to me. After the excitement of the snow going and the cards being sent to me from Mr No one, work had to be done with moving the hen houses. I wrapped up well and went out with Mr Milner. No sooner had we got up to the end of the garden and through the gate into the orchard beyond when we were swooped on by the magpie. It flapped onto my shoulder, then to the ground and onto Mr Milner's back again. He said, 'It talks. it said, "What are you doing?"'

Well, Mr Milner hadn't believed me, but it was true. We decided to look over the hedge next door which divided Mr Milner's orchard from the allotment of his neighbour.

We looked and looked in disbelief. Someone had made a mound of earth about eight feet high and on the top was a fence. We could see someone sitting on the top and looking with a telescope over to us. He must have been looking for the bird. We were finding it a bit of a nuisance. Mr Milner was trying to hit it with his cap or his spade, and I was shouting for him to leave it alone. The chap next door was raving, waving his telescope in the air and shouting abuse at us, so we had to go back in and leave things as they were.

There were jobs to do. The post office letter box had to be opened from inside the shop. All the letters were taken out and put on the table and I or Mr Milner would frank them with a special post office stamp with a date and 'Papplewick' on it over the postage stamp. Really, it was a pleasant job. In between people would want serving.

It was a nice job till one day when it was my turn to open the letter box. I got the letters out and a bunch of keys fastened onto a pile of letters. I just thought someone had posted a letter and dropped their keys in.

Mr Milner decided to have a closer look and found a letter addressed to him to call the police. We had the local policeman on his bike come round to investigate. There were several more plain clothed police in the evening and next day. We were told one of the villagers, a man, had committed suicide. Before doing so, he had left letters and keys posted in the letter box for Mr Milner the postmaster to send the letters to whom they were addressed. By the time the post box had been opened at 4.30 in the afternoon, the poor sad man was dead.

For all of us it wasn't over. We three had to have a sit down with the chief of CID to make statements and have our finger prints taken, though we were the innocent parties. The incident was finished after four or five days so we were able to get on with the general day's work.

We still had our, or next door's, magpie to contend with. I got so that I daren't go out into the back garden. Of course I had to make an effort as the bucket with a wooden seat lavatory was outside; we all had to use it. The bird would swoop over and I felt as though it was coming for me. I really felt I wanted to say things to it. Did it really talk? I kept thinking.

More peculiar things were going on over the hedge, what with the heap of soil and a castle like fence on the top. There were other happenings.

I had heard some banging; it sounded like bricks being knocked with a hammer. From my bedroom window, where I had seen the pig being killed. I could see the man swinging a hammer at his lavatory bricks. He had already taken his slate roof off and was, brick by brick, knocking it down. I watched him a few minutes every day, until one day when the building was halfway down. It was raining fast. I looked over and he was sitting on his bucket and wooden seat with his umbrella up to keep dry. I ran down to Mr and Mrs Milner and we three had quite a laugh. They both 'laffed' but I 'larfed'. 'Laff' was how they spoke in the Midlands. The funny part of it was that the lavatory was shared with the house the other side of him. It was quite funny for us, but the poor man I realised afterwards couldn't help his mental condition.

There had been five brothers living in the house next door, none of whom were married. Once a week they would take it in turns to scrub the tables and chairs and leave them outside to dry. One day I saw the settee and two armchairs outside; they had been cleaned down but it had rained. They had left them out for a day or two to dry.

These brothers had worked on local farms and one had worked for the council. He pushed a barrow with a shovel and yard brush and he kept clean the pavements and roads of Papplewick. The grass edges were kept neatly trimmed. There wasn't a piece of rubbish in sight. He would have a good word for everyone. The story was that when he got paid along with his brothers, any money left would be put in a tin chest. The tin chest was full of gold sovereigns but after they died it was never found. I really thought the one who was left, who owned the magpie and made the high mound with the fence like castle on the top, had buried it under his make-believe castle.

The magpie was really a nuisance to us. He would fly over as soon as we opened the back door. He would come in on Monday washday and would follow me out to help put the washing up. For me it was the last straw when he flew on the line and pecked at the pegs till they came out and the washing dropped in the muddy soil, so it had to be washed again. That Monday was the last day the bird was seen. No one knew where it had gone. But I believe it went the same way as Mr Milner's dog a few years before.

I'd had a letter from Mum and Dad. They said they hadn't had any more flying bombs as the British, Americans and Canadians had invaded France a few months before. They had now captured and destroyed the launch pads. Mum said she had heard the war would soon be at an end. Germany was being attacked from both the French side by the Allies and the Russians on the other side of Germany.

She wrote and said it was time I came home.

My days of evacuation were nearly over and I could get a job and earn some money. I wrote back to say I was so afraid of the doodlebugs and V2s. I would wait a little longer, I didn't say I was seeing Ronald.

After Easter, April time 1945, Mrs Milner said it was perhaps time I went home. She said she didn't want to be responsible for me any more.

I was very upset. They didn't want their little evacuee any more. I cried for days as I had grown to love the village and all the people. To go back to London where no one knew me was awful.

The end of April brought some wonderful news from Germany. Over the wireless it was given out that Hitler, the head of the German nation, had committed suicide.

Every day from the end of April 1945 the wireless was on all day for news of the war. We heard Russians had gone to invade Berlin. Oh! How I remembered praying for the Russian soldiers as they were fighting in mud and snow with very little food a few years earlier. Also all the Australians, Canadians, New Zealanders, American and British were still fighting the Japs. That war was to go on till 14 August 1945.

On 7 May 1945 our war in Europe was at last over. The Germans had waved their white flag. I was to go home now, back to

London, after some very happy yet hard working years. I was no more a little evacuee. Back I went to the bright lights.

The blackouts had been taken down from the windows, but the rationing was to remain the same for some time. The end of the European war didn't mean we could get plenty of oranges, bananas and other foods. They came through into the shops gradually through the months ahead.

The 8 May 1945 saw lots of singing and dancing in the streets. I had said my goodbyes to my war-time friends, but I did promise to see them again. My young man Ronald came to London with me to meet my family, though he already knew them a little. He came for the VE celebrations, and what fun they were.

There were sirens and bands playing around Trafalgar Square. Lord Nelson on his column must have felt very proud of us winning the war.

Thousands of people were all joining arms and dancing to the music. Balconies and windows were full of people waving flags and blowing horns. The celebrations went on all night and for days afterwards until we were all exhausted. This little evacuee had had her day.